DATE		

APULEIUS AND

The Golden Ass

1. The Prologue to *The Golden Ass*. This manuscript (F) is the earliest authority for Apuleius' novel and was written in the eleventh century at Monte Cassino. Biblioteca Medicea-Laurenziana, Florence (Ms. laur. Plut. 68.2, c. 126). Photograph by Guido Sansoni.

APULEIUS AND
The Golden Ass

JAMES TATUM

Cornell University Press

ITHACA AND LONDON

Cornell University Press gratefully acknowledges a grant from
the Andrew W. Mellon Foundation that aided in bringing
this book to publication.

First published 1979 by Cornell University Press.
Published in the United Kingdom by Cornell University Press Ltd.,
2-4 Brook Street, London W1Y 1AA.

International Standard Book Number 0-8014-1163-7
Library of Congress Catalog Card Number 78-74220
Printed in the United States of America
*Librarians: Library of Congress cataloging information
appears on the last page of the book.*

PA
6217
.T3

TO

JACK HARVEY

CATHERINE CHAPMAN

ROB REYNOLDS

BEST OF TEACHERS

Contents

8 / Contents

Illustrations

Preface

The frontispiece to this book reproduces the Prologue to Apuleius' *Golden Ass* as it appears in a manuscript now in the Laurentian Library, Florence. Modern textual criticism has established this manuscript as the most authoritative source of the novel. It was written at the monastery of Monte Cassino in the latter part of the eleventh century. Giovanni Boccaccio may have borrowed it for his own use; certainly he knew Apuleius' novel and adapted some of its tales for the *Decameron*, which he began writing in 1348. This manuscript is of particular importance because, in addition to being the authority for Apuleius' *Golden Ass*, *Florida*, and *Apology*, it is also bound with our only source of Books 11–16 of Tacitus' *Annals* and the beginning of his *Histories*. In the second line the reader will notice the superscription "Ego salustius emdavi rome felix" ("I, Sallustius, corrected [this] at Rome happily"). We know from a later scribal note that this Sallustius was not the Christian scribe of this volume (who, as usual, is anonymous), but the editor of a codex from the end of the fourth century. Sallustius reports he read and corrected the text during the consulships of Olybrius and Probinus and, later, of Caesarius and Atticus. Since the Romans identified calendar years by the names of their consuls, Sallustius was at work in A.D. 395–397. These dates place him only two hundred years after the death of Apuleius himself.

The manuscript now known as Codex 68.2 of Florence vividly demonstrates why classical studies take the directions they do. It is a familiar theme to classicists—but perhaps one not so easy to appreciate in these days of mass printing—that we have only a few tenuous threads to connect our own world with that re-

11

mote one in which Apuleius lived and wrote. Much can be done and has been done to bring such works as Apuleius' novel to later readers, and in many more ways than could easily be summarized. Scholarly interests and needs can change a great deal, and so can readers' tastes. The reasons the anonymous scribe copied Sallustius' codex may not be the ones that led Sallustius to make his edition. The purpose of this book can be stated simply enough.

My aim is to show how *The Golden Ass* can be related to Apuleius' other literary activities. These activities are not generally familiar and may be more remote from most of us than the works of Euripides or Vergil. After an interpretive essay on the novel, I shall attempt to explain the nature of Apuleius' artistic life in the second century. Supplementary appendixes will acquaint readers with his *Florida*, with genuine magic spells from the Greek magical papyri, and with another devotee's prayer to Isis.

Since I hope to reach not only classicists but also those readers who may not be acquainted with the ancient novel, I have addressed the book to what is usually called the general reader; but in truth the later second century is not a time overly familiar to many teachers of Latin and Greek. I hope my colleagues will forgive me for saying what to them may be obvious. My intention has been to discourage no fewer readers than I have to.

To that end all passages are quoted in translation (my own unless otherwise noted), with the original only where it seems needed. I am grateful to Georg Luck, Bryan Reardon, Gerald Sandy, and Ken Dowden for reading earlier drafts of this book and offering advice on many points; to J. Gwynn Griffiths for generous help with the translations in Appendix 2; to the two anonymous readers for Cornell University Press; and to Barbara Salazar and her colleagues in the editorial department of the Press. I alone am responsible for any errors that may remain.

Permission to reproduce photographs for the illustrations in this book has kindly been granted by the Biblioteca Medicea-Laurenziana, Florence; the Deutsches Archäologisches Institut, Rome; the Rijksmuseum van Oudheden, Leiden; B. G. Teubner GmbH, Stuttgart; F. W. Goethert, Berlin; the Musée du Louvre,

Paris; the Bibliothèque Nationale, Paris; the Museo Archeologico, Florence; and the Trustees of Oberlin College. I am also grateful to A. D. Leeman for permission to quote from *Orationis ratio*; to Fabian Opeku for permission to consult his University of London dissertation on the *Florida*; to Samuel Stevens Hakkert and Company for permission to quote Vera F. Vanderlip's translation of the First Hymn of Isidorus; and to the University of Wales Press, Cardiff, to quote from J. Gwyn Griffiths' translation of Plutarch's *On Isis and Osiris*.

A fellowship from the president and trustees of Dartmouth College in 1972–1973 enabled me to begin research on this book. I had the good fortune to do so at the Institute of Classical Studies at the University of London. My special thanks to E. W. Handley and the staff of that institution for the exemplary hospitality they show every visitor to Gordon Square. I must also acknowledge the many courtesies shown me by the Warburg Institute and the pleasure of working in its remarkable library. Catherine Frasier and Deborah Hodges typed the first and final drafts of something more often a palimpsest than a manuscript, and Evelyn Marcus supplied the line drawings that accompany the text.

JAMES TATUM

Hanover, New Hampshire

Explanatory Note on Classical Citations

References to poetic texts give line numbers only (e.g., *Menaechmi* 1–4) or, in the case of longer works, book and line numbers (e.g., *Odyssey* 12.184–191). For prose texts matters are more complicated. Generally the conventional citations permit fairly precise reference to prose authors—but not quite so precise as to poets. For Apuleius' works, the following system is used: for *The Golden Ass*, book and chapter number (e.g., 4.6); for the *Apology* and *On the God of Socrates*, chapter numbers only (e.g., *Apology* 32; *On the God of Socrates* 12); and for the *Florida*, only the number of the selection in that anthology (e.g., *Florida* 17). References to other prose texts will include author, English title, and book and chapter number where appropriate (e.g., Cicero, *First Oration against Catiline* 3–4; Augustine, *On the City of God* 18.18). For certain Greek authors, specific references follow the pagination and section numbers of standard editions of their works; e.g., Plato, *Republic* 5.457C indicates Book 5, page 457, section 3 in the edition of Henri Estienne (Stephanus), published in 1578. Traditional Latin titles appear only in the index, after the author's name or the English title of his work.

APULEIUS AND

The Golden Ass

CHAPTER 1

The Sophist as Novelist

Originally men applied the term "sophist" not only to excellent orators of brilliant reputation but also to philosophers who fluently expounded their teaching.

—Philostratus, *Lives of the Sophists* 484.

The arts of Apuleius the sophist are very much in evidence in his lone novel, *The Golden Ass*, or *Metamorphoses*.[1] It is possible he made at least one other attempt at writing in what was for his day an unusual genre, but virtually nothing of *Hermagoras* survives.[2] *The Golden Ass* had a better fate: from the time it was written, in the latter decades of the second century, it has been widely read—and from a number of perspectives. These are not always perspectives that Apuleius himself might have understood. Of particular interest have been the tale of Cupid and Psyche (Books 4–6) and the account of Lucius' conversion to Isis (in Book 11). Since many readers today may not recognize what is implied when I speak of Apuleius as a sophist, some reference to his participation in the intellectual life of the second century is desirable.

Apuleius was born during the reign of Hadrian, about A.D. 125, in the North African town of Madauros. Like other prominent literary figures of his time, he never had cause to regret his

1. The manuscript tradition indicates that *Metamorphoses* (or *Eleven Books of Metamorphoses*) was the original title of the work. The more familiar *Golden Ass* is a translation of *asinus aureus*, a colloquial phrase meaning "the first-class ass" or "darling donkey," and I shall use this second title throughout.

2. *Hermagoras* might be a philosophical dialogue. Its six fragments (only isolated words and sentences quoted by late grammarians) are collected in Jean Beaujeu, *Apulée: Opuscules philosophiques* (Paris, 1973), 170–172.

provincial origins. This was an age that afforded exceptional opportunities for talented and ambitious *littérateurs* who excelled at entertaining audiences throughout the empire. These writers are now known generally as the sophists, but such other titles as *rhetor* (orator) and even *philosophos* (philosopher) were equally popular.[3] Apuleius himself preferred to be called a philosopher, perhaps because of his master Plato's strictures about sophists. His gifts for philosophy and rhetoric carried him far beyond his modest beginnings, to Carthage, Athens, and Rome. All his writings reflect a cultural ideal that had animated the work of Roman authors since the time of the Scipios: mastery of the Latin language combined with a broad knowledge of the poets and prose stylists of Greek literature. Save that Latin was his primary language, his career was indistinguishable from that of a Greek sophist such as Aelius Aristides. Apuleius likewise combined the arts of the rhetorician with the superior wisdom philosophers liked to claim.

To modern eyes this background may not seem a likely apprenticeship for a novelist, but from what we can glean from Apuleius' other writings, the novel simply gave his talents a more ambitious scope than was possible in the most popular literary form of his day: epideictic, virtuoso oratory. *The Golden Ass* displays the same religious and philosophical scruples as his more conventional works. In its language and style, the novel reflects the dazzling rhetorical arts of the sophist. Only that skill with the spoken word was now applied to an essentially different art form.

Like other novels of antiquity, *The Golden Ass* reminds us in many ways of Homer's *Odyssey*. That poem often served as a paradigm for novelists in antiquity. Apuleius tells of the strange and marvelous adventures that befall a young man because of his desire to know. Very early in the novel this desire fixes obsessively on the arts of magic. In this way Lucius' *curiositas* sets his story somewhat apart from other classical romances, in which an erotic bond between hero and heroine is the dominant

3. G. W. Bowersock, *Greek Sophists in the Roman Empire* (Oxford, 1969), 110–117.

theme. In the latter part of Apuleius' work the parallel between the "curious" Lucius and Odysseus is drawn quite explicitly (9.13). Curiosity gives an intellectual yet reprehensible tinge to the character of Lucius. He reveals his disquiet at being taken for a *curiosus* by his very first words in the novel: "On the contrary, do share your story with me. I'm not so much nosy as one who only wants to know everything—or about as much as I can" (1.2).

At the same time *The Golden Ass* is so varied a work that it resists an easy reading. The novel requires detailed critical description. Studies of its sources have established that Apuleius based his novel on a Greek tale about a young man transformed into an ass. An epitome of that same story appears in the form of Lucian's satirical novella *Lucius or the Ass*.[4] To this original story Apuleius then added a great many other episodes and tales, and he rounded the whole work off with a final book, which recounts Lucius' conversion to the cult of Isis. In the final pages, Apuleius himself appears; evidently he and his hero are the same person (11.27). Little wonder that scholarly opinion has been mixed in its estimation of the success of his efforts. Most specialists are now willing to take the eleven books of *The Golden Ass* as a unified work of literature, despite earlier scholarly objections to some slips and inconsistencies in the narrative. Analytical critics based their arguments mostly on differences between Apuleius' novel and the Greek novella. Such discrepancies as they have found do not constitute a grave obstacle to the enjoyment of Apuleius' novel, whether it is read in Latin or in translation.

A matter less easy to resolve is the novel's mixture of entertainment and moral instruction. *The Golden Ass* is religious propaganda of a very sophisticated type. The lofty conclusion in Book 11 accords with what we know of Apuleius' pretensions elsewhere to being a "serious" (i.e., philosophical or religious) author. But many aspects of the novel cannot be said to be quite

---

4. Photius, a Byzantine scholar of the ninth century, attributed the original story to "Lucius of Patrae" (*Library*, 129), but nothing by this Lucius survives; see the introduction to and translation of *Lucius or the Ass* in M. D. Macleod, *Lucian*, Loeb Classical Library 8 (London, 1967), 47–145.

so earnest. Apuleius is a witty writer equipped with an unusually sharp sense of irony and a well-developed taste for the ridiculous. His narrative often wanders off into episodes and tales that only the most resolute of commentators would fail to smile at—or be shocked by.

A close reading of *The Golden Ass* will show that the humor and frivolity of this comic novel are of a peculiarly narrow range. These qualities become apparent as soon as we have fixed in our minds the substance of each of the eleven books. There is abundant evidence that Apuleius shaped each of them into a discrete unit, and these original divisions of the story can make a considerable difference in our perception of the whole work. This is one point that has often been overlooked, as for instance in Graves's translation and in Grimal's commentary on the Cupid and Psyche story.[5] These are only slight discourtesies, and alternative divisions of any text may have their uses. But to begin with, let us be sure we understand Apuleius' arrangement of things before we try to impose a scheme we think is better.

5. Robert Graves, trans., *The Transformations of Lucius, Otherwise Known as The Golden Ass* (London, 1950); Pierre Grimal, *Metamorphoseis 4.28–6.24: Le conte d'Amour et Psyche* (Paris, 1963).

CHAPTER 2

Eleven Books of Metamorphoses: A Guide to Some Basic Aspects of the Novel

> Nor was any solace forthcoming for my tortured life unless it was that I was refreshed by my innate curiosity; for no one paid any attention to me, all freely said and did whatever they wished. Not undeservedly did the divine author of ancient poetry among the Greeks, when he wished to portray a man of the greatest intelligence, sing of one who attained the highest virtues by travel to many nations and knowledge of all kinds of people. I for my part render thankful thanks for the time I spent as an ass; after I was hidden in its skin and had experienced all kinds of fortune, it restored me to my original form—if none the wiser at least knowing many things.
>
> —Lucius to his reader (9.13)

If a reader were to inspect such a manuscript for Apuleius' novel as the one descended from our friend Sallustius, he would not see the words *Asinus aureus—Golden Ass*—but such a rubric as "Book 2 of the *Metamorphoses* of Apuleius" or a scribal notations such as "Book 1 of the *Metamorphoses* is ended and now Book 2 starts" (*Metamorphoseon lib. I Expl. Incip. II*). "Eleven Books of Metamorphoses" will probably never replace either *The Golden Ass* or *Metamorphoses* as a title for the novel, but these words describe precisely its structure and its distinctive quality as a work of fiction; hence it is a title appropriate for at least this chapter. For the essence of *The Golden Ass* is that no event or character in it can be trusted to remain what it may at first seem to be. Nothing that is said—even by the narrator—can be taken at face value.

Even the most elementary guide to such a work, then, poses

an obvious problem, and I must stress that the present chapter is nothing more than that, an introductory essay to some basic aspects of the novel. It is not only a question of what to retain and what to leave out—though that is hard enough to decide fairly—but also whether these remarks might better be offered in a continuous interpretive essay or proceed book by book. Chiefly because of existing studies, which make it unnecessary to go back over the same ground in the same way, I have decided to follow the second approach. Since P. G. Walsh has provided a detailed explication of the novel tied to a continuous summary of its plot, and since earlier scholars have followed the same approach, the most useful strategy seems to be to give readers of this book some sense of the drama and surprise with which Lucius' story unfolds.[1] What I mean by the words *drama* and *surprise* will be apparent when we explore some major themes of the novel.

Fortune and curiosity, *fortuna* and *curiositas*, are two words that describe basic aspects of Lucius' life and personality, and he eventually comes to loathe the very sound of them (7.2–3, 11.23); but this is not apparent in Book 1. Magic and its mysteries are dangerous, a kind of bastard antireligion that causes much evil in the world by reversing the natural order of things for the benefit of only those who practice it; but again, Lucius does not quite realize this in Book 1. To take up a more positive theme: the single reliable way our souls may find salvation is by the intervention of a superior being, one strong enough to turn aside malign Fortune and offer us a haven. Yet, once again,

---

1. P. G. Walsh, *The Roman Novel: The Satyricon of Petronius and the Metamorphoses of Apuleius* (Cambridge, 1970), 141–189. The following books, addressed to the specialist, offer interpretations of Apuleius' novel by detailed comparisons with his possible Greek sources and the later picaresque novel: Paul Junghanns, *Die Erzählungstechnik von Apuleius' Metamorphosen und ihrer Vorlage, Philologus*, suppl. 24, Heft 1 (Leipzig, 1932); Hermann Riefstahl, *Der Roman des Apuleius* (Frankfurt, 1938); Rolf Heine, "Untersuchungen zur Romanform des Apuleius von Madaura" (diss., Göttingen, 1962); Helmut van Thiel, *Der Eselsroman:* vol. 1, *Untersuchungen;* vol. 2, *Synoptische Ausgabe* (Munich, 1971–1972); Ettore Paratore, *La novella in Apuleio*, 2d ed. (Messina, 1942); and Gerardo bianco, *La fonte greca delle metamorfosi di Apuleio* (Brescia, 1971).

Lucius does not come to this realization until he reaches that "safest of all harbors," Cenchreae, the scene of his conversion in Book 11 (10.35). A growing number of critical essays have analyzed such themes as these; they have enabled readers of *The Golden Ass* to unify in their own minds an extraordinarily complex text.[2] But perceiving thematic unity is only one way of understanding Apuleius. None of these studies was intended to be a substitute for a reading of the novel and participation in Lucius' odyssey. As a tour de force that deliberately misleads the reader, this work may be compared with *Tristram Shandy*.

What I propose, then, is to offer the briefest of summaries of each of the books, indicating the major points by chapter number, with as much discussion as is necessary to bring out basic points of interest in each book. Clarity and conciseness are the aims. Apuleius employs many stock characters and situations, and although they are repeated for a definite artistic purpose, in the later books of the novel adulterous wives proliferate to such a degree that the narrative seems to be repeating itself. It is as if three or four comedies of Plautus were being performed at once. Since this device might be taken as a sign of Apuleius' lack of artistic discipline, an interpretation with which I cannot agree, I feel that the more concise our orientation, the better.[3] For the sake of clarity, some cross-references to earlier or later passages will be required, but as much as possible this chapter will be a guide in the sense that it will reflect what it is like to follow Apuleius' tale as it unfolds.

2. A number of critical essays elucidate the major themes of the novel; among the most important are Gertrude Drake, "Candidus: A Unifying Theme in Apuleius' *Metamorphoses*," *Classical Journal* 64 (1968, 102–109; Antonie Wlosok, "Zur Einheit der Metamorphosen des Apuleius," *Philologus* 113 (1969), 68–84; Carl C. Schlam, "The Curiosity of the *Golden Ass*," *Classical Journal* 64 (1968), 120–125; Gerald N. Sandy, "*Serviles Voluptates* in Apuleius' *Metamorphoses*," *Phoenix* 28 (1974), 234–244; Brendan Kenny, "The Reader's Role in the *Golden Ass*," *Arethusa* 7 (1974), 197–209; and J. L. Penwill, "Slavish Pleasures and Profitless Curiosity: Fall and Redemption in Apuleius' *Metamorphoses*," *Ramus* 4 (1975), 49–82.

3. See Graham Anderson, *Studies in Lucian's Comic Fiction* (Leiden, 1976), 34–67.

BOOK 1

A Greek of distinguished background promises to entertain us with tales of magical transformations (1). The story then begins with his visit to Thessaly on business. On his way into the city of Hypata, he meets two other travelers, who are in the middle of an animated conversation. Our narrator's first words reveal him to be eager to learn anything and everything possible (2). His interest focuses rapidly on a miraculous story told by one of the travelers, Aristomenes (5–19). Aristomenes once had a friend named Socrates, who trifled with the affections of an old woman named Meroe, a witch who used occult powers to punish faithless, reluctant lovers (7–10). Sometime during the night, before the two men could flee from her wrath, Meroe and her sister Panthia broke into their lodgings, cut out the heart of Socrates, and replaced it with a sponge (12–13). Socrates seemed for a time to have miraculously escaped from the witches' power (17–18), but the next day, as he leaned over a stream to drink, the wound gaped open and he fell lifeless to the ground (19). Aristomenes' unnamed companion scoffs at the tale from beginning to end (3, 20), but our narrator appears to believe every word he hears and is now eager to learn more about magic (20). He arrives in Hypata and stays at the house of a family friend, Milo, a garrulous miser with a wife named Pamphile (21–22). Near the end of Book 1 he meets Pythias, an old friend from student days in Athens, who appears to have been transformed into an officious brute by his office as aedile in charge of public food supplies (24–25). At the very end of Book 1, as he recounts his bizarre meeting with Pythias, the narrator's name is at last revealed to be Lucius.

Apuleius' Dialogue with His Reader

A Greek tale this may be, but the opening of *The Golden Ass* is rich in its evocations of earlier Latin literature. In one way, it resembles a prologue to a Roman comedy. Altogether traditional in Plautus, for example, are such devices as the outline of an intricate plot, the hope that the audience will find what it is about to hear entertaining, and the elegant apology by the nar-

2. The setting of Lucius' travels in Greece, from Hypata in Thessaly to Cenchreae and the isthmus of Corinth.

rator for any shortcomings in his eloquence. Compare the prologue to Plautus' *Menaechmi* (5–10):[4]

> nunc argumentum accipite atque animum advortite:
> quam potero in verba conferam paucissima.
> atque hoc poetae faciunt in comoediis:
> omnis res gestas esse Athenis autumant,
> quo illud vobis Graecum videatur magis,
> ego nusquam dicam nisi ubi factum dicitur.

> Now take down this plot and pay attention: I'll relate it all with
> as few words as I can. Poets do this anyway in their comedies.
> "Everything takes place in Athens," as they say, so that it may
> seem all the more Greek to you. *I'll* tell nothing unless it's a fact
> that is told.

The *ego tibi* with which the novel opens also resembles the
sermo or conversation typical of Roman verse satire; both Horace
and Juvenal engage their readers in one-sided conversations.
The Golden Ass, in contrast to the works of Petronius and the
Greek novelists, is distinguished by just such a dialogue between its narrator and reader. More than once the story pauses
while Lucius elicits a hypothetical question from us:

sed forsitan lector scrupulosus reprehendens narratum meum sic ar-
gumentaberis: "unde autem tu, astutule asine, intra terminos pistrini
contentus, quid secreto, ut adfirmas, mulieres gesserint, scire
potuisti?"

But perhaps you the exacting reader of my tale may find fault with what
I've said and object: "Now just how is it, my clever little ass, that, even
though you were shut up inside the mill, you were able to hear (as you
declare) what the women were carrying on in secret?" [9.30]

Elsewhere he anticipates our objection that a philosophical di-
gression has gone on too long:

4. See Warren Smith, Jr., "The Narrative Voice in Apuleius' *Metamorphoses*,"
Transactions and Proceedings of the American Philological Association 103 (1972),
513–534; for further advice on the writing of *exordia,* see Quintilian 4.1.

sed nequis indignationis meae reprehendat impetum secum sic repu-
tans: "ecce nunc patiemur philosophantem nobis asinum," rursus,
unde decessi, revertar ad fabulam.

But lest someone should find fault with my righteous outburst and so
think to himself, "Behold, now we're to endure a philosophizing ass,"
I'll go back and pick up the story where I left off.   [10.33]

He also forestalls a question we might be about to raise:

quaeras forsitan satis anxie, studiose lector, quid deinde dictum, quid
factum; dicerem, si dicere liceret, cognosceres, si liceret audire.

Perhaps you would inquire anxiously, then, my careful reader, what
happened after that, what was done: I would say so if it were permitted
me to say; you would know if it were permitted for you to
hear.   [11.23]

Obviously, the way in which Lucius' *sermo* unfolds is a constant challenge to the reader's wit and sense of parody. We must
remember that this is a novel in which we do not even learn the
name of the main character until very near the end of Book 1;
and then it appears only as if by accident, as a vocative in the
words of his friend Pythias: *mi Luci*, my dear Lucius (1.24).[5]
Furthermore, since the "conversation" of Roman satire owed no
little of its distinctive ironic flavor to the master of the dialogue
himself, Plato, it should come as no surprise that in the first
book of this novel we find a parody of one of the works of the
very *divinus vir*, or godlike man, Plato, whose name Apuleius
was pleased to claim for his own epithet.

In the tale of Aristomenes, Socrates—a singularly misnamed
fellow—comes to the disastrous finale of his adventures in a
setting suspiciously like the one Plato describes at the opening
of the *Phaedrus*. He and Aristomenes stop for lunch on the

5. The technique of late-naming is characteristic of Apuleius; cf. the introduction of Charite's name at 7.12, of Psyche's at 4.30, and of Apuleius' own name at
11.27 (though quite indirectly, as only a "poor man from Madauros" is mentioned). See Blanche Brotherton, "The Introduction of Characters by Name in the
Metamorphoses of Apuleius," *Classical Philology* 29 (1934), 36–52.

banks of a pleasant river, in the shade of a plane tree. But the setting for the beginning of one of Plato's great dialogues becomes in Apuleius only the sorry resting place for Aristomenes' pathetic friend (cf. Plato, *Phaedrus*, 229A–B, with 1.18–19). Plato's Phaedrus goes wading in the Ilissus; then Apuleius' Socrates gets to drop dead in it. This is a text that makes as many demands of its readers as any novel one could name from the modern period.[6]

The Meaning of "Metamorphoses"

The prologue's references to a "Nilotic reed" and an "Egyptian papyrus" are not so much a literal apology for writing materials as sly allusions to the home of the Isis cult.[7] But since these are only hints about the surprising conclusion in Book 11, we should see now exactly what is meant by the Greek word *metamorphōsis*.

Metamorphosis and conversion have traditionally been regarded as two distinct experiences. The first belongs exclusively to myth and literature. The transformation of human beings into beasts or inanimate objects is a fantastic subject, a favorite theme with all kinds of literary artists, and understandably so. Metamorphoses impose a just, ironic interpretation about a person's life that is as compelling in the earliest stories of the classical tradition, in Homer, as it is in the more recent tales of Kafka and Roth. Conversion, on the other hand, has always been recognized as an action rooted in the world of experience. It is a dramatic turnabout, a change—sudden or gradual—that can be observed and analyzed like any other human activity. Although it was first singled out as an ideal means of education in philosophy,[8] conversion now is more familiar to us as a phenomenon

6. See Wayne C. Booth, *The Rhetoric of Fiction* (Chicago, 1961), and Wolfgang Iser, *The Implied Reader: Patterns in Communication in Prose Fiction from Bunyan to Beckett* (Baltimore, 1974).

7. For a detailed analysis of this aspect of the novel, see Piero Scazzoso, *Le metamorfosi di Apuleio* (Milan, 1951).

8. E.g., the discussion of conversion (*epistrophē*) in Plato, *Republic* 7. 518B–D; see Paul Aubin, *Le problème de la "conversion"* (Paris, 1963), 49–68.

of the psychology of religion; for example, the conversion of Saul on the road to Damascus. A. D. Nock's famous study of the subject includes a long summary of Lucius' conversion in Book 11; and indeed Book 11 is the most extensive and detailed account we have of a turn to a new life in a pagan religion.[9]

So much scholarly literature has developed about each of these experiences, and for the most part developed separately, that it may be difficult now to imagine a very close association between the two; yet *The Golden Ass* confronts us with a conversion that is apparently only one final instance of metamorphosis. The logic of this connection is easy to see. "Metamorphosis" is literally a change of form, "conversion" a change of soul. In *The Golden Ass* the first phenomenon leads inexorably to the second—from a narrative that has been the exclusive concern of the literary scholar to one that the historian of religion has marked as his own. But in this novel no sharp distinction need be drawn between metamorphosis and conversion; indeed, the text of *The Golden Ass* does not require us to separate the two. In Book 11 metamorphosis simply serves as a metaphor for spiritual change.[10]

One other aspect of metamorphosis should be emphasized. Metamorphosis is usually brought about by a person's thoughts and actions; that is, the cause of such transformations may be discovered in the psychology of the person transformed. There is also a strong element of poetic justice—and sometimes of poetic injustice—so that the transformation becomes a summary judgment on a person's life. Metamorphosis occasionally may come as a reward; more often it is a penalty. In the *Phaedo*, Plato has Socrates explain that a soul may be imprisoned in a body that corresponds to the character of its former life. Socrates' interlocutor, Cebes, asks for some examples of metempsychosis as a punishment:

9. A. D. Nock, *Conversion* (Oxford, 1933), 138–155.
10. Compare the general theme of transformations of body and fortune (1.1) with the scene of Lucius' retransformation (11.14–16); for a more detailed study of metamorphosis, see James Tatum, "Apuleius and Metamorphosis," *American Journal of Philology* 93 (1972), 306–313.

"What kinds of character do you mean, Socrates?"

"The kinds who have cultivated gluttony and violence and drunkenness and have not taken pains to avoid them are likely to assume the bodies of asses and other animals of that sort. Or do you not think so?"

"Yes, I think that is quite likely."

"And those who have preferred lawlessness and tyranny and robbery take on the bodies of wolves and hawks and kites. Where else can we say such ones go?"

"By all means, that is where they go."

"Then indeed," he said, "is it clear where all the others go, each of them according to the way they have spent their life?"

"Yes, that is clear," he said.   [*Phaedo* 81D–82A]

I shall return to the idea of metamorphosis as a kind of punishment in my remarks on Book 3. For the moment it is sufficient to realize that the less familiar (but original) title of the novel, *Metamorphoses*, announces that we may expect radical transformations in appearance but, curiously, *not* in character. Generally speaking, tales of transformation will be not so much about the development of a person's psychology as a *symbol* of it; some single facet of the personality will be represented in a symbolic transformation. In this act lies the philosophical aspect of which Socrates speaks in the *Phaedo*. Lucius will turn into an animal that represents the very faults he possessed as a young man: unwise curiosity, audacity, and sexual license.[11] Lucius, with a man's intelligence, will be encased within the body of a beast and never change his character at all; he will continually fall prey to the same errors as when a man, and, because of his shape, those errors will be grosser than ever.

Reference to another *Metamorphoses* in Latin literature reveals

11. These are the main qualities of the character Lucius in Lucian's *Lucius or the Ass*; for a discussion of the folkloric aspects of these traits, see Alexander Scobie, *Apuleius Metamorphoses (Asinus Aureus): vol. 1, A Commentary* (Meisenheim am Glan, 1975), 26–46.

a similar connection between character and transformation. To mention one of the first instances of metamorphosis in Ovid's poem: Lycaon slaughters and cooks human flesh for Jupiter and as punishment is transformed into a wolf—the beast he already was in all but appearance: "Still Lycaon, though, the same grayness, the same savage face, red eyes, a very image of bestial savagery" (1.238–240). There are gentler and happier metamorphoses throughout Ovid's poem; the range of his theme is so broad that his perpetual song (*carmen perpetuum*) carries him through virtually all of Greek and Roman mythology, down to an apotheosis of Julius Caesar and a rather enthusiastic anticipation of the same honor for Augustus (15.849–870).[12] There is a similar climax in the exaltation of Lucius in Book 11, though in every other respect Apuleius is far less compendious than Ovid.

By contrast to other people he meets on his travels, Lucius may seem abject indeed; but his psychological state is enviable. He will maintain the character he had when in human form. Others less fortunate will suffer extreme spiritual transformations through a disastrous passion of one sort or other, and with consequences as spectacular as any metamorphosis; hence the psychological condition of a person's soul is the factor that determines the new shape engendered by metamorphosis. Change of outward appearance only typifies the psyche within. In this sense, metamorphosis easily embraces the religious experience once given classic definition by William James:

> To be converted, to be regenerated, to receive grace, to experience religion, to gain an assurance, are so many phrases which denote the process, gradual or sudden, by which a self hitherto divided and consciously wrong, inferior and unhappy, becomes unified and consciously right, superior and happy, in consequence of its firmer hold on religious realities. This is at least what conversion signifies in general terms, whether or not we believe that a direct operation is needed to bring such a change about.[13]

This is precisely Lucius' experience in Book 11. There are many other violent psychological transformations in *The Golden Ass*,

12. See G. K. Galinsky, *Ovid's Metamorphoses* (Berkeley, 1975), 42–70.
13. William James, *The Varieties of Religious Experience* (New York, 1917), 189.

such as those of Charite and the cruel landlord.[14] Only Lucius' change is joyful and enduring.

In the opening sentence of the novel, Apuleius describes the continuity of transformations as a single phenomenon affecting body and soul alike:[15] "... figuras fortunasque hominum in alias imagines conversas et in se rursum mutuo nexu refectas" ("figures and fortunes of men changed into other appearances, then restored again by a common twist back into their original selves"). This is a more elaborate theme than the comparatively simpler statement that opens Ovid's poem, because it links the theme of metamorphosis with the additional idea of fortune's varied and unpredictable ways.[16] Fortuna in Apuleius is synonymous with Tyche, the Greek goddess traditionally regarded as the power that changed one's fortunes, now this way to good, now that way to ill. By his opening words linking *figurae* and *fortunae*, Apuleius prepares the way for his story to lead directly to the Isis Tyche, or Fortuna videns, of Book 11; there we shall see the Hellenistic goddess of fortune assimilated to Isis (11.15).[17] As the aretalogy of Isis from Kyme concludes, Isis is the goddess who conquers fate (in Greek, *heimarmenē*); fate obeys her.[18]

As if with the first words of an epic poem (e.g., *arma virumque cano*), then, Apuleius has announced a complex theme that unites all eleven books of his novel. The evil deeds of Meroe and Panthia in Book 1 are linked directly to the benign magic of Isis in Book 11. There is one other kind of metamorphosis that also

14. See 8.11–12, 9.35–38, and especially 10.24, on the transformations of a jealous wife; she moves rapidly from unjustified suspicions of adultery by her sister-in-law to hatred to torture and murder.

15. *Conversio* in the more restricted sense of a purely moral change is a familiar feature of Christianity (e.g., Augustine's discussion of conversion to the one true and holy God in *On the City of God* 8.24); see Nock, *Conversion*, 212. In this sense the transformation of Lucius into an ass is as much an act of religious symbolism as it is a theme in folklore.

16. Cf. Ovid, *Metamorphoses* 1.1–2: "In nova fert animus mutatas dicere formas Corpora" ("My aim is to tell of shapes changed into new bodies").

17. See Siegfried Morenz, *Egyptian Religion* (Ithaca, 1973), and John Gwyn Griffiths, *Apuleius of Madauros: The Isis-Book (Metamorphoses, Book XI)* (Leiden, 1975), 241–244.

18. Werner Peek, *Der Isishymnus von Andros und verwandte Texte* (Berlin, 1930), 124.

deserves our attention. It is to the literary transformations of Apuleius that we now must turn.

The Witty Tale

Somehow and in some way Apuleius made a Greek novel into a Latin novel. As we observed in Chapter 1, exactly what his Greek sources may have been and exactly how he achieved his transformation remain difficult and unsolved questions. We know he was working with a model—but what model? "Lucius of Patrae" and his *Metamorphoses* are elusive bibliographical citations; *Lucius or the Ass*, while clearly related to the basic story of Books 1–10 of *The Golden Ass*, is simply that: a relative, to be sure, but whether a cruel stepmother or only a gentle maiden aunt we do not yet know.

Given these circumstances, it is important to realize that Apuleius faced a problem that confronts any literary artist working with a model. In adapting a narrative for one's own purposes, or in adding new material, one always runs the risk that the final product may be undigested and, for at least some of the prospective audience, indigestible. This problem is at least as old as Homer. A notorious instance of the difficulties involved in the interpolation of a story into a frame narrative is the speech of Phoenix in the ninth book of the *Iliad* (9.430–619). It is undeniably one of the great moments in the poem, yet it betrays in numerous ways both the poet's efforts to integrate it into the fabric of the epic and some inevitable failures to do so.[19] In his long speech, Phoenix tells his former pupil what he ought to (but does not) do; indeed, his words so much foreshadow the tragic consequences of Achilles' obstinate refusal to reenter the war that that fact alone has caused some Homerists to condemn it as a later interpolation.

It is not entirely clear that Homer was really nodding in Book 9, but the parallel should be enlightening to every reader of Apuleius. We may approach his text from an analytical point of

---

19. See Denys Page, *History and the Homeric Iliad* (Berkeley and Los Angeles, 1959), 297–315; for a more recent assessment of the problem and references to the extensive literature on Phoenix's speech, see Judith A. Rosner, "The Speech of Phoenix: *Iliad* 9.434–605," *Phoenix* 30 (1976), 314–327.

view; or, on the other hand, we may attempt to appreciate as best we can the final results of his literary stitchwork. Neither approach is superior to the other, though partisans for each one may try to say so.[20] Readers of this book will find themselves seated in a Unitarian congregation.

Apuleius employs many witty devices throughout his Greek tale. For example, Lucius has a horse named Candidus ("Whitey"), who is mentioned at the very beginning of his travels (1.2); he reappears near the end of the novel, when Lucius has been transformed back into a man and has chosen a new life in the service of Isis (11.20). This is another instance of Apuleius' subtlety. The white horse, like the parodic allusions to the setting of the *Phaedrus* in Aristomenes' tale, recalls Plato's myth of the charioteer in the same dialogue (cf. *Phaedrus* 246A–B and 253D–255A); there the white thoroughbred that tries to soar to heaven represents the soul striving to flee what is base and ignoble in life. Lucius will attain such a state of grace in Book 11, and the return of the white steed Candidus symbolizes that transformation. Here is something that will amuse both the connoisseur of Plato and the student of the novel.

The tales that appear throughout the first ten books are Apuleius' most conspicuous innovation (when we compare his novel to the epitome *Lucius or the Ass*). All of them are cast with considerable sensitivity to the major themes and characters of the novel. The first one, by Aristomenes (1.5–19), illustrates the dangers inherent in Lucius' desire to learn everything he can. If it is not too confusing to speak of such a thing in a novel usually termed "comic," curiosity might even be said to be Lucius' tragic flaw. His disclaimer at 1.2 is not enough to free him from the charge. Such an idle, malicious curiosity was condemned by many authors before Apuleius. In Theophrastus, it is said to be the sort of character trait that leads a son to go up to his father to tell him that his mother is already asleep in bed (*Characters* 13). The perils brought about by the curiosity of the ass also give the moral tag that ends *Lucius or the Ass* (56).

When curiosity leads one to pry into the secrets of religion, of

20. See C. M. Mayrhofer, "On Two Stories in Apuleius," *Antichthon* 9 (1975), 68–80.

course, it tends to be less amusing. The failing of curiosity is thus not to be confused with the more exalted desire to learn that distinguishes the philosopher from other people—though Lucius *sounds* like a philosopher in Book 1. Nor have we to do with anything like the scientific curiosity of the Platonist and naturalist Apuleius. Plato had already explained that an unquenchable desire to know was a quality that set the lover of wisdom, the philosopher, apart from every other man (e.g., *Republic* 5.475C).[21]

In the epigraph to this chapter, we can see easily the mock-heroic way Lucius compares himself to Odysseus. In point of fact, a serious point lies beneath that jest; ancient interpreters of the *Odyssey* regarded curiosity as Odysseus' great shortcoming.[22] They had some justification: the temptation of the Sirens, the song that nearly destroyed Odysseus, was the temptation of knowledge:

Come sail this way, much-praised Odysseus, great glory of the Achaeans, stay your ship and give an ear to our song. For no man ever sails past here in his black ship before he has heard the sweet voice from our lips; he takes his delight in it and sails on with greater knowledge. We know all the toil that the Argives and Trojans endured in wide Troy at the will of the gods; we know all things that happen upon the fruitful earth.   [*Odyssey* 12.184–191]

But to balance this dangerous curiosity, Odysseus and Lucius have a compensating virtue: *tlemosyne,* or endurance. If both of them are nearly destroyed by their zeal to learn, they also enjoy the favors of a goddess who will enable them to endure and survive trials no one else can.[23] Of course the full significance of *curiositas* is disclosed only gradually in the novel; indirectly in

21. As is explained in Chapter 4, this ideal is the cornerstone of Apuleius' own defense in his *Apology.*
22. Philo Judaeus (ca. 30 B.C.–A.D. 45) is a particularly important source for the middle Platonists' conception of curiosity; cf. the remarks later in this chapter on Book 11, and the priest's speech at 11.15.
23. Not surprisingly, a basic theme of the *Odyssey* is the seemingly incorrigible stupidity of some human beings; see Zeus's speech, the first in the poem, on the folly of Aegisthus (1.28–43).

Lucius' experiences, more explicitly in the tale of Cupid and Psyche.

Because Lucius' perception of *curiositas* comes to him only gradually—the reader will recall our strategy of following the novel as it unfolds—I have drawn attention to this pervasive theme only to emphasize that it is to that very typical quality in Lucius that the first of the tales of *The Golden Ass* appeals.[24] Lucius wishes to know everything or as much as possible, and the story he hears from Aristomenes at once focuses that desire on magic. For in Aristomenes Lucius encounters someone who not only believes in magic but also has experienced it at firsthand. And as a storyteller Aristomenes is no mean rhetorician; his tale is tailor-made for Lucius' innocent ears. His unnamed companion scoffs at the story and likens it to nothing more than a string of impossible conjuring tricks. But within the tale the character Socrates recites an identical number of supernatural powers, as if to contradict the skeptic:

This lie is no more true than if somebody could by a magic incantation make swift rivers turn back, thicken the sluggish sea, still the winds to silence, stop the rising sun, plunge the moon from the sky, strip away the stars, take away the day, make it everlasting night.   [1.3]

Ah, she's a sage powerful, who can make the sky fall, hold up the earth, freeze springs, wash away mountains, raise the dead, weaken the gods, put out the stars, light up Tartarus itself.   [1.8]

Similarly, Lucius tells how he nearly choked on some cheese he had eaten the day before, and Aristomenes finishes *his* tale by telling how Socrates collapsed dead after quenching his thirst from eating cheese (cf. 1.4 and 1.19).

These disagreeable coincidences give a certain imbalance to the world of actual experience. There is a logic to it all, but it is the logic of a nightmare. Already Lucius is in a world in which he cannot quite trust in the sanity of events around him. Toward

24. For an essay that emphasizes the didactic aspect of this and other tales, see James Tatum, "The Tales in Apuleius' *Metamorphoses*," *Transactions and Proceedings of the American Philological Association* 100 (1969), 487–527.

the end of the book, when Phythias grinds Lucius' fish into the market pavement,[25] that feeling is intensified. It may well be that Lucius' desire to know everything resembles the noble urge of the philosopher; it may be that he is content to let each person's fortune work out as it will. But he has set about pursuing that hidden knowledge in a world that from the start is exposed as vicious and, as the encounter with Pythias shows, not even sane.

BOOK 2

The next morning Lucius awakens more eager than ever to learn the secrets of the magic arts that Aristomenes has described (1). He is oblivious of the moral implicit in a startlingly lifelike sculpture depicting the punishment through metamorphosis meted out to Actaeon for his curiosity (4). He is equally unmoved by the warnings of his aunt Byrrhena about the magic arts of Milo's wife, Pamphile (5). He resolves to discover the secrets of magic by ingratiating himself with the servant girl Fotis (6) and is soon deep in a passionate affair with her (7–10). She inspires a remarkable meditation on women's hair (2.8). Later, in the course of a dinner-table conversation with Milo and Pamphile, we learn that a certain Chaldean prophet, Diophanes, had predicted Lucius' future fame and fortune (12). The nature of that fame and fortune is not now revealed. Finally, at a drunken party Lucius hears yet another strange tale, this time about Thelyphron, a man who was once paid to guard a corpse from witches and in doing so suffered humiliation and mutilation for refusing to heed warnings about the power of magic (21–30).

25. The episode was singled out by Erich Auerbach for its disquieting departure from "reality"; see his *Mimesis: The Representation of Reality in Western Literature* (Princeton, N.J., 1953), 60–63. Since fish were said to have devoured the parts of Osiris that Seth cast into the Nile, the encounter with Pythias may be a subtle nod toward Egypt, like Apuleius' "Nilotic reed" (1.1) and the priest Zatchlas who appears in the next book (2.28). See Ph. Derchain and J. Hubaux, "L'affaire du marché d'Hypata dans la 'Métamorphose' d'Apulée," *Antiquité classique* 27 (1958), 100–104.

Lucius stumbles drunkenly home and at the door to Milo's house slays what he believes to be three bandits trying to break in (32).

Three Fair Warnings

In his growing obsession to learn the *ars magica*, Lucius reflects a common superstition that magic can create a universal sympathy between animate and inanimate things. It now seems as if the whole world about him has been transformed by a magic incantation (2.1). His interest in magic focuses entirely on metamorphosis and, we must note, with no regard whatever for any of its more sinister uses. In Books 2 and 3 he pursues a reckless course that reveals two faults Greek philosophers and theologians regarded as causes for the downfall of the soul: a curiosity to know about divine matters and a bold resolve to indulge that curiosity no matter what the cost. Platonists and Gnostics followed Plato's lead in attributing these faults to the voluntary choice of each soul itself, for which god was blameless (e.g., *Republic* 10.617E).[26] *Tolma*, or rashness, is indeed as much a facet of Lucius' personality as his curiosity. It is reflected in the notably higher tensions of Book 2. One warning about magic is followed by another, each more strident than the last, yet Lucius heeds none of them.

The implication of the sculpture depicting Actaeon's metamorphosis into a stag escapes him completely, even though it is explicitly interpreted as a punishment of curiosity. Actaeon had looked at a sight forbidden to men to see, and for this transgression, says Lucius, he is about to be punished by metamorphosis. (In this overtly didactic reading, by the way, Apuleius differs from Ovid, who described Actaeon as blameless, a victim of the worst kind of bad luck; see *Metamorphoses* 3.141–142). Lucius himself will soon watch Pamphile's "mysteries," and the consequence of that particular contemplation will be scarcely less pleasant. The irony grows a little heavy-handed when Byrrhena tells Lucius that "everything you see is

---

26. See A. J. Festugière, *La révélation d'Hermès Trismégiste:* vol. 3, *Les doctrines de l'âme* (Paris, 1953), 63–103.

yours." Every reader must realize that it is not only Byrrhena's house that belongs to Lucius (2.4-5).

Similar dramatic irony characterizes Lucius' announcement at the dinner table that evening that he will enjoy a great reputation: some day he may be the subject of "a great history, an unbelievable tale, the theme of whole books" (2.12). His host, Milo, follows this declaration with a tale of his own experience with a Chaldaean prophet, Diophanes, a man who by coincidence happened to predict Lucius' coming fame and fortune. As with the less-than-Socratic Socrates of Book 1, Diophanes, whose name means "message" or "revelation from God," does not quite live up to his title. Milo tells how Diophanes lost out on an important business deal with a businessman named Cerdo (Greek for "profit") because he blurted out a tale of all his disasters at sea—a veritable odyssey, Diophanes said (*Ulixea peregrinatio,* 2.14). Again the irony is monumental; if Diophanes did so badly for himself, what may we expect of the nature of Lucius' own great history? Surely, Milo declares, Lucius will be an exception, an improvement on Diophanes' dismal record. In reality, Lucius seems to be sinking deeper and deeper into matters he does not really understand. Whether his innocence is merely stupidity or something more profound is a matter we shall return to at a later point.

In the same way, Thelyphron's tale is more than it may at first seem. In one sense it is a splendid entertainment, if sadistic in some details. In another sense it is a parable of what can befall a heedless, rash soul possessed by an impulse to take foolish and needless risks. Thelyphron ("Weakwit") personifies *tolma,* and is an implicit warning about that particular failing in Lucius. Thelyphron's experience also shows that magic can be very costly for the unwary. In his tale there appears the first of a series of faithless and murderous wives who will turn up all too often in Lucius' later adventures. In this instance it is one who poisons her husband on their wedding day. There is a waft of Egyptian (Isiac) religion when an Egyptian prophet, Zatchlas, appears and exposes her crimes for all to see. The final outcome of the case is understandably of less interest to Thelyphron—at least his fellow guests do not give him an opportunity to reveal it.

In Zatchlas (a name of uncertain meaning, possibly related to the Greek *sōs*, safe) we recognize a godlike man—a *theios anēr*, as the Greeks would call him—who can help the good, punish the wicked, and even raise the dead. He is an eloquent witness to the existence of beneficent gods, though at this point no name of any deity is mentioned. Yet when a shaved, berobed priest swears by the *sistra Fariaca*, the Pharic or Egyptian rattles used in the ceremonies of Isis' cult, he identifies himself very clearly as a servant of Isis. In the midst of all these ominous rumblings, even as the world of magic is about to close in on Lucius, Apuleius sounds a clear note of possible salvation by the appearance of Zatchlas, that "Egyptian prophet of the first rank" (2.28). The contrast between Zatchlas and the incompetent Diophanes underscores this point.

BOOK 3

The next morning a guilt-stricken Lucius is dragged to trial for his alleged murder of three citizens of Hypata (1–2). After a notably eloquent effort by Lucius to clear himself (3–6), the three "bandits" are revealed to be nothing but wineskins (9). The whole episode is part of Hypata's festival to Risus, the god of laughter; Lucius has been an unwitting participant in the celebration (11). Pamphile's maid, Fotis, later confesses that she and her mistress had brought the wineskins to life by a mistake in their magic spells (13–18). Lucius' passion to learn the secrets of Pamphile's art rises to its highest pitch. Fotis reluctantly reveals the mysteries of her mistress' arts, and he is allowed to witness the transformation of Pamphile into an owl (19–21). He hastily rubs himself with an ointment that he thinks will work a similar change on him, but to his horror he is transformed into an ass. Fotis has supplied him with the wrong potion (24). Before he can restore himself to human form with the antidote of roses, he is abducted by a band of robbers who break into Milo's house (28).

A Mirror Held Up to the Reader

If *The Golden Ass* was written after Apuleius delivered his *Apology* (A.D. 158–159), the opening of Book 3 was a nice joke

3. Isis with a sistrum in her right hand. Museo Capitolino, Rome. Cf. Figure 11. Reproduced by permission of the Deutsches Archäologisches Institut, Rome. Photograph by Anderson.

between him and those of his readers who knew about his trial at Sabratha. The motif of false accusations recurs several times later in the novel (especially notable outbursts will come at 7.2–3 and 10.33). The courtroom debate is also a favorite scene in the works of such Greek novelists as Chariton and Achilles Tatius.[27] There may even have been an actual festival such as is described in Apuleius' novel, but neither the type scene nor the historical reality of the god Risus is of present concern.[28]

The most important artistic function of the Festival of Laughter is that it serves as a kind of play-within-a-play, dramatizing the true nature of the comedy of *The Golden Ass*. We know that Apuleius was fascinated by the interplay between stage comedy and the comedy of life; as he notes in the *Florida*, the difference between what we suppose to be merely a *fictum argumentum*, or fictional plot, and the *vera fabula* of real life may not always be so substantial as we think.[29]

This affinity between the "entertainment" of fiction and the setting in which it is told characterizes Apuleius' novelistic technique. One has only to recall the disturbing echoes of the tales of Aristomenes and Thelyphron in Lucius' own experience: more than a little of that fiction turned into fact. Similarly, most of the novel's comic effects depend on the humiliation and suffering of its characters, and all of the books except the last are marked by the same mixture of sadism and terror, comic desperation and reversals of fortune that are celebrated at the opening of Book 3. But here we catch a glimpse of Apuleius' view of his audience and of its reactions to his version of the human comedy. The Festival of Laughter holds up a mirror to readers of the novel; in the *Schadenfreude* of Lucius' tormentors we may see a reflection of ourselves.[30]

---

27. See Thomas Hägg, *Narrative Technique in Ancient Greek Romances: Studies of Chariton, Xenophon of Ephesus, and Achilles Tatius* (Stockholm, 1971).

28. There are references to a Greek god of laughter (Gelos) in Plutarch, *Lycurgus* 25.4 and *Cleomenes* 30.1, and Aulus Gellius, *Attic Nights* 1.24.3.

29. See the translation of *Florida* 16 in Appendix 1.

30. As a student of Platonic doctrine, Apuleius would know his master's discussion of the important role that malice (*phthonos*) plays in comedy; see *Philebus* 47B–50E.

Lucius' Initiation into Magic and the Symbol of the Ass

The remainder of Book 3 is devoted to the initiation of Lucius into the *disciplina* of magic. It is a bastardized version of the religious experience he will undergo in Book 11. Appropriately named, Fotis shows Lucius only too clearly that magic is capable of working great changes in a person's life.[31] The *disciplina* of Pamphile is no mere superstition running counter to the laws of the natural world; it exists as a demonic counterpart to the beneficent power of Isis and is now exposed as something far more substantial than the basis of a good tale. In the Greek magical papyri, for example, a spell calls on the power "which fills all things with its light and which with its particular power shines throughout the entire universe."[32]

The Greek magical papyri also give us a glimpse of something we may presume would have been anathema to devotees of Isis: prayers to Seth, who is depicted as a man with the head of an ass (note the letters CHΘ, or Sēth, written across his chest). Plutarch, in *On Isis and Osiris* 31, says that this demonic being murdered Isis' brother-consort, Osiris, and that worshipers of Isis represented him through the shape of such beasts as the crocodile, the hippopotamus, and the ass:

Osiris and Isis thus changed from good daemons into gods. The weakened and shattered power of Typhon, which still gasps and struggles, is appeased and mollified by them partly by sacrifices, while at other times again they humiliate and insult it in certain festivals, jeering at men of ruddy complexion and throwing an ass down a precipice, as the people of Coptos do, because Typhon had a ruddy complexion and was asinine in form. The people of Busiris and Lycopolis do not use trumpets at all because they make a noise like an ass; and they believe the ass to be in general not a pure, but a daemonic beast because of its likeness to Typhon, and when they make round cakes in the festivals of

31. Her name is related to the Greek *phōtizein* (derived from the noun *phōs*), meaning not only "to shine" but also "to fill with light"; see Rudolf Bultmann, "Zur Geschichte des Lichtsymbolik im Altertum," *Philologus* 97 (1948), 1–36.

32. Karl Preisendanz, ed., *Papryi Graecae Magicae: Die griechischen Zauberpapyri*; 2d ed., ed. Albert Henrichs (Stuttgart, 1973–1974), vol. 1, 106. For a discussion of magic conceived of as a religion in classical antiquity, see Franz Cumont, *Oriental Religions in Roman Paganism* (New York, 1956), 182–195.

4. Seth on a Greek magical papyrus. Reproduced from Karl Preisendanz, ed., *Papyri Graecae Magicae: Die griechischen Zauberpapyri*; 2d ed., Albert Henrichs (Stuttgart, 1973–1974), vol. 2, Plate 2, Illus. 11, by permission of B. G. Teubner GmbH, Stuttgart, and Rijksmuseum van Oudheden, Leiden.

the months of Paÿni and Phaophi, as an insult they stamp on them an image of a tied ass. In the sacrifice to Helius they instruct those who venerate the god neither to wear golden objects on the body nor to give gold to an ass.[33]

The ritual of the Isis cult thus provided a constant reminder of Seth-Typhon; every evocation would naturally be representative of a life of evil opposed to Isis.[34]

Plutarch goes on to say that Seth was subdued for a time but

33. J. Gwyn Griffiths, *Plutarch's De Iside et Osiride* (Cardiff, 1970), 165.

not entirely; for devotees of Isis, he remained forever an opposing force, a master of evil changes, the source of a good deal of
the evil in human lives. The cult of Isis and Osiris is thus distinguished by a dualistic opposition of demonic, magic powers.
Seth exists as a divine creator of evil, independent of Isis, a creator of good.

The ass that appears in Figure 4 may help us see why Apuleius
chose to cast his odyssey toward Isis into what may at first seem
a bizarre form.[35] The transformation of a man into an ass is not
only a matter of poetic justice; for those who know the cult of
Isis, it also is an action of the highest religious significance. That
is, the transformation of Lucius is one of the most compelling
religious experiences in the novel—fully as significant as his
much-studied conversion in Book 11. We must try to see this
aspect of the scene in Book 3 if we are to grasp the sense in
which reading *The Golden Ass* could be a philosophical and religious as well as a literary experience. In discussing some equally
unfamiliar aspects of early Roman religion, Georges Dumézil
explained the need to take religious symbols seriously, no matter how strange they may at first appear:

Symbolization is the basic resource of every system of thought, every
articulate or gestural language. It is what permits one, if not to voice, at
least to approximate, to delimit the nature of things, by substituting for
the stiff and clumsy copula of identity, "to be," more flexible affinities:
"to resemble," "to have as attribute or principal instrument," "to recall
by an important association of ideas." Consider the cross in many
oratories, the rudimentary crucifix on which the Christ is not shown but

34. It is possible that even the color of the "golden ass" has religious significance; see René Martin, "Le sens de l' expression asinus aureus et la signification
du roman apuléien," *Revue des Etudes Latines* 48 (1970), 332–354. Martin suggests
that the ruddy complexion that Plutarch mentions in describing Typhon is what
is signified by the Latin adjective *aureus. Aureus,* golden, would then be a translation of the Greek *pyrrhos,* ruddy or flame-colored. Even if Martin is correct, his
argument does not affect the clear priority of the title *Metamorphoses.*
35. See the unkind remarks about Lucius at 6.24–26, 7.21, 9.42 (the proverbial
curiosity of the ass), 10.13–17 (the gluttony of the ass), and especially 10.20–22
(the prurience of the ass); on prurience, see Jean Hian, "L'Ane d'or d'Apulée et
l'Egypte," *Revue de Philologie* 47 (1973), 274–280.

which is merely two pieces of wood placed at right angles. If someone from the outside, who does not know of Christianity or wishes to make fun of it, should see this, how would he judge the often burning devotion of which this cross is the object? As a variety of "dendrolatry": these pieces of wood, it might be said, are holy, they emit *mana*, etc. Of course we well know that it is an entirely different matter: the simplest cross conjures up the Passion, the scheme of salvation, from the Incarnation to the Redemption, Adam with the tree of sin and Jesus with the tree of forgiveness. The fervor of the suppliant is not directed to the material object, but to the historical realities and to the dogmas which the Gospels and theology associate with the agony of Calvary. The pieces of wood are only an aid, a means of recall, precious and even holy to the degree that while it "recalls" is precious and holy.[36]

In Dumézil's terms, the ass reminds us of the comparable agony of Osiris and, somewhat like a cross, represents the agency of that suffering.

In Book 11, Isis herself will condemn the notion of this loathsome beast, the *detestabilis belua* (11.6), though neither she nor anyone else in the novel will ever actually pronounce his name.[37] A worshiper of Isis would thus find the description of Lucius' metamorphosis into an ass more than something to marvel at:

After assuring me of these matters time and time again, she crept into Pamphile's bedroom with great trembling and removed a little box out of its chest. I hugged and kissed it, praying that it would give me a prosperous flight. I tore off all my clothes and, sticking my hand in greedily, applied a large handful to every part of my body. Then with my arms outstretched and flapping I made movements like a bird. Neither down nor feathers appeared, but my hair hardened into bristles, my tender skin roughened into hide. All my toes and fingers lost their habitual number and were forced together into single hoofs; from

36. Georges Dumézil, *Archaic Roman Religion* (Chicago, 1970), vol. 1, 26–27.
37. Seth-Typhon is never mentioned because of the fear that pronouncing his name might cause him to appear, or in some other way invoke his power (contrast the éclat of "Queen Isis," *Reginam Isidem*, at 11.3, and see the discussion of that passage in Chapter 5); see Martin P. Nilsson, *Geschichte der Griechischen Religion*, 3d ed. (Munich, 1967), vol. 1, 55–56; and cf. the frequent use of Seth's name by someone who does want to invoke his power in the prayers of Appendix 2.

the end of my spine a long tail grew forth. Now my face became enormous, my mouth widened, I had gaping nostrils and drooping lips; my ears bristled aloft to an excessive length. I could perceive no consolation for this wretched metamorphosis, unless it was that I was enlarged beyond Fotis' capacity to deal with me. Now quite past all help, as I looked over my body I saw that I was no bird but an ass, and I complained of Fotis' deed; but since I was deprived at once of human gesture and voice, all I could do was stick my lip out and pout at her sideways with watery eyes, silently upbraiding her. [3.24]

A transformation at once amusing and ghastly: there is no difficulty in seeing it as simple poetic justice for all of Lucius' rashness and curiosity; we must not overlook the fact that the ass was proverbially ridiculed in folktales and folk sayings for its lust, its curiosity, and its generally gross habits.[38] But devotees of the Isis cult would read a more sinister meaning into the metamorphosis. As Plutarch's account shows, this scene would also summon no little revulsion. Eventually Lucius will discover a goddess who will dispel all but the memory of his transformation—but not until Book 11. In this respect, while we may note many sly and puzzling allusions to the rituals or legends surrounding the cult of Isis, we must appreciate that none could possess quite the horror of this passage.

Let me state the case another way: What would it be like if in *The Pilgrim's Progress* the hero, Christian, were transformed into Apollyon, so that the object of salvation became for a time a symbolic representative of Satan himself? Apuleius achieves a very similar effect with the metamorphosis scene that gives *The Golden Ass* its name.

BOOK 4

Lucius is often tempted to elude his captors, but he prudently stops short at the last moment on seeing one of his less wise fellow pack animals thrown over a precipice (5). When he finally reaches the bandits' mountain lair (6), a robber arrives to report

38. See Scobie, *Apuleius Metamorphoses*, vol. 1, 26–46.

the death of three heroes of the band—Lamachus, Alcimus, and Thrasyleon (9–21). All three have met gory and spectacular deaths in the line of duty and are cherished as models for all bandits to live by. No sooner is that speech ended than a beautiful young maiden is brought in; she has been abducted on her wedding day, her husband slain in giving chase (23). To comfort her, the drunken old woman who serves the bandits begins a long tale of consolation about the similar fate of a beautiful young girl named Psyche (28). So beautiful was she that the worship of Venus herself was neglected (29). For this insult to her divinity Venus punished Psyche by asking her son Cupid to cause Psyche to fall in love with the basest and ugliest of living creatures (30–31). Psyche is then isolated from all men, who look upon her almost as a goddess, perfect and unattainable (32). Appropriately for this *sermo Milesius,* her parents ask the oracle of Apollo at Miletus for an opinion; Apollo's Latin verses decree that Psyche must be left alone on a rock for her husband, who will take the form of a raging serpent (33). Everyone thinks the poor girl has been ruined by her beauty, and she is left on a remote mountain rock to die (34). Then gentle Zephyrus comes along and carries Psyche away to a valley sprinkled with flowers, far from the rocky crag (35).

A Joke Becomes Reality

The three bandits whom Lucius attacked in Book 2 were only products of wine and magic. But as happens constantly in *The Golden Ass,* the fantastic and unbelievable have become real. At the end of Book 2 Lucius had thought he was defending Milo's home against three bandits; now in Book 4 he is not only a captive of genuine bandits but is very shortly to hear tales of their exploits. It is fair to warn the reader that even these three tales anticipate later events in the novel.

The three stories of banditry say much about the inspiration of the bandits—and their gullibility. Their weakness, so nicely exposed here in the long speech of one of their fellows, will prove fatal when the disguised husband of the young maiden appears in Book 7. Thus the tales about Lamachus (the name of an Athenian general at Syracuse) and Alcimus ("Strong Man") impress us mainly with the imprudence of these two heroes. The first is so incautious as to have his hand nailed to a door; the second is pushed out of a window by a weak old woman. The third, Thrasyleon ("Bold Lion"), is the most ingenious. With the aid of a clever disguise he manages to convince a rich man, Demochares ("Crowd Pleaser"), and his household that he is a trained bear. Thrasyleon's difficulty is that he is too good at his trade. When he tries to escape his new owner, he is slain after a heroic struggle. For all practical purposes he may as well have been metamorphosed into a bear; the disguise is not discovered until the household servants begin to skin the "bear's" carcass. In effect, these tales of banditry function as elaborate puns on basic themes of the novel. Alcimus' fortunes (that is, luck) take a bad turn because he thinks only of the "fortunes" (that is, money) of others and believes everything that he hears (4.12). Thrasyleon dies because he is too successful in the metamorphosis of his disguise (4.21).

The Drunken Old Woman's Story

The famous tale of Cupid and Psyche begins deceptively as a fairy tale, an attempt to console the captive maiden. Typically, the maiden is not named until Book 7, where her "eloquent name," Charite, is pronounced with great effect (7.12). In her telling of the tale it is soon apparent that the drunken old woman is well versed in Latin poetry: the wrath of Venus having been aroused by the slight done to her beauty, she pursues her victim, Psyche, with the relentlessness of Juno in the *Aeneid*. Although Venus' opening words are reminiscent of the language of Lucretius,[39] the substance of her speech is a thematic reworking of Juno's first speech in the opening of Vergil's poem; there Juno complains of the slights she has suffered from the Trojans and of the scant honor paid to her divine image.[40] Venus is similarly offended by Psyche. In a sardonic twist to the

39. *De rerum natura* is recalled in such phrases as *rerum natura parens, alma Venus*, and *elementorum origo initialis*. See Walsh, *Roman Novel*, 55 and note.

40. *Aeneid* 1.34–49, a speech already parodied by Ovid. See *Metamorphoses* 3.262–272, in which Juno uses Vergilian Latin to complain of Jove's *amores* rather than of the somewhat loftier transgressions of Aeneas and the Trojans.

traditional theme of the judgment of Paris, she wonders what winning that contest accomplished for her after all. While Apuleius' Venus uses some of the words of Lucretius, this shrew is no *Aeneadum genetrix*; for similar language in a more decorous setting, compare 4.34 with Isis' words at 11.5.

There is more to Apuleius' Venus than her variation of epic diction. After Book 5, the name Fortune is not mentioned in the story, as Venus and Fortune become for a time identical. This merging of identity in Book 6 makes Psyche's tale parallel to Lucius' own story; if he began his travels with scarcely any care for Fortune's ways, he will soon come to feel very differently about her (see 7.2-3). Apuleius achieves a significant variation of the typical polarity existing in the Greek novel between the goddess of love and the goddess of fate: between the blind Tyche, who drives lovers over land and sea, and the benign Aphrodite, who unites them in the end.[41] Although Lucius is driven from pillar to post, so to speak, Apuleius, rather than depicting him or Psyche as moving from the power of Venus to the power of Fortuna, has combined the influence of both goddesses into one inferior, "earthly" affliction that enslaves men and makes their lives little better than those of beasts. Ultimately, in contrast, a seeing Fortune, Fortuna videns, will be combined with a heavenly Venus, whom Apuleius describes in his *Apology* as the goddess who ennobles those who worship her and allows no base pleasures of the flesh.[42] Of course Isis is that power.

As for the situation in the bandit's cave, Apuleius leaves matters in suspense; he closes Book 4 with Psyche in the same perilous situation as the young maiden who is hearing the tale. The only hint of what is to come is that we know she awaits some winged monster "before whom even the gods quail" (4.33). A reader with even a smattering of Plato would recognize that "monster" as Cupid.[43]

41. This polarity has long been a recognized feature of the ancient novel; see Erwin Rohde, *Der griechische Roman und seine Vorläufer*, 3d ed. (Leipzig, 1914), 296.

42. Cf. the remarks of Phaedrus in Plato, *Symposium* 180D-E (on Uranian (Heavenly) and Pandemic (Earthly) Aphrodite), with *Apology* 12.

43. See the description of Eros' powers in Plato, *Symposium* 178A-179B.

BOOK 5

Psyche is wafted by Zephyrus to the jewel-encrusted home of her new husband (1). Servants minister to her, fulfilling her every desire; but they are unseen, she hears only their voices (2-3). Cupid comes to her at night, makes her his wife, and departs before dawn (4). Her husband tells her that she is never to be permitted to look at him (5) and warns her three times of the dangers of fortune and the evil snares of her jealous sisters (6, 11, 12), but she gradually gives way to their plots and at last resolves that she must discover his identity (18-21). When she sees Cupid in all his glory by lamplight, she is overwhelmed by his beauty (22); but a drop of oil from her lamp spills out and burns the shoulder of her sleeping husband (23). He flies away angrily, vowing never to look on her again (24). Psyche takes revenge on her evil sisters by tricking each one into leaping off a cliff in the hope of being carried by Zephyrus to Cupid (26-27); then she sets out on a long journey to find her husband. In the meantime Venus learns that her son has disobeyed her orders to destroy Psyche; she ignores the pleas of Juno and Ceres that she forgive the young lovers (31).

The Old Woman's Tale Becomes an Allegory

From the opening of Book 5 we seem to have lost for a time the main thread of Lucius' story; yet as we proceed it becomes increasingly obvious that a lengthy and ambitious fable is unfolding which has more and more bearing on our interpretation of the novel.[44] In Book 4 we appeared to be hearing a tale of consolation in which the happy reunion of a husband and wife was foretold. Now, in Book 5, aspects of Psyche's story begin to appear as unmistakable traits of Lucius', above all the element of curiosity. Since we are dealing with a myth about characters who personify soul (*psyche*) and desire (*eros* or *cupido*), we only gradually recognize the scope of Apuleius' ambitions. Such a

44. Especially recommended for discussion of this part of the novel are Pierre Grimal, *Metamorphoseis 4.28-6.24. Le Conte d'Amour et Psyche* (Paris, 1963); and Walsh, *Roman Novel*, 190-223.

5. Cupid and Psyche embracing. Museo Capitolino, Rome. Reproduced by permission of the Deutsches Archäologisches Institut, Rome. Photograph by Alinari.

tale can make a statement about the human condition and the possibilities for our salvation and happiness.

Now the insouciance with which the old woman began her story in Book 4 did not provide the slightest hint that such a philosophical and religious myth was in the offing (as we shall see in Chapter 4, philosophy and religion were for Apuleius virtually the same thing). Yet is this strategy not entirely in keeping with what we have already observed of his narrative style? Throughout the novel he begins stories as if innocently unaware of where they will ultimately lead. In the tale of Cupid and Psyche, that technique is at its most subtle and elusive.

As in the interpretation of any allegory, much depends on which key one thinks unlocks which door. In this instance the possibilities for confusion are abundant, since scholars have demonstrated that Psyche's search for her husband is an elaborate construction of episodes reminiscent of the sacred legend of Isis and Osiris.[45] The tale evokes well-known Platonic myths and doctrines, especially the myth of the soul in the *Phaedrus* (246A–257B) and the teaching of Diotima in the *Symposium* (201D–212C).[46] There are also echoes of the Cinderella folktale in the episodes of Psyche's wicked, jealous sisters.[47] Controversy has raged for nearly a century over which of these aspects should be emphasized at the expense of all the others, but our present reading of Apuleius' tale does not depend on unraveling the tangled skein of sources that may lie behind it. We need only to realize that three distinct meanings exist not so much in conflict as in complementary relationship to one another. The tale is first of all a kind of folktale of conjugal fidelity rewarded, as the ending of the story in Book 6 optimistically predicts the eventual reunion of husband and wife. Psyche's abiding curiosity—first

45. This aspect is heavily emphasized by Reinhold Merkelbach, *Roman und Mysterium in der Antike* (Munich, 1962), 1–90. Many important earlier studies of the tale, representing diverse points of view, are collected in Gerhard Binder and Reinhold Merkelbach, *Amor und Psyche* (Darmstadt, 1968); for a lucid reassessment of the whole problem, see Detlev Fehling, *Amor und Psyche* (Mainz, 1977), 11–28.

46. Carl C. Schlam, "Platonica in the *Metamorphoses* of Apuleius," *Transactions and Proceedings of the American Philological Association* 101 (1970), 477–487.

47. For bibliography on the folktale, see J. O. Swahn, *The Tale of Cupid and Psyche* (Lund, 1955), and Scobie, *Apuleius Metamorphoses*, vol. 1, 15–18.

to know the identity of her husband, then to know the contents Proserpina's jar—also marks her as an allegorical figure who possesses Lucius' distinguishing characteristic. Finally, as suggested earlier, the names of the characters point us toward the most significant meaning of all. A myth about Soul and Love can pose a universal statement about all human souls, all human desires. For an understanding of this highest or at least most abstract level of meaning, some further explanation will be helpful.

Cupid: The Nature and Function of a Daimōn

Cupid is not always the pudgy cherub familiar to us from St. Valentine's Day, though he was of course sometimes so depicted in artistic monuments in antiquity. In the view of the Greeks, Eros was also an intermediate being or *daimōn* between gods and mortals.[48] As such Eros was perceived as a power or force (*dynamis* in Greek, *potestas* in Latin) that enabled the human soul (*psychē*) to be bound in love to the gods. The Greeks' conception of Eros as *daimōn* is as old as Hesiod (*Works and Days* 122). Apuleius' treatise *On the God of Socrates* is his exposition of Plato's teaching about *daimones*, in a literary style appropriate to the tastes of his Latin-speaking audiences. We may let the author of *The Golden Ass* explain in his own words the nature and function of a *daimōn*:

It is not a task for the gods of heaven to descend to things here below. This lot befalls the intermediate gods, who abide in those regions of the air that are adjacent to the earth and no less so on the borders of heaven, just as in every part of the world there are animals peculiar to that part—in the air those that fly, and on the ground those that walk. [*On the God of Socrates* 7–8]

Cupid's role is that of an intermediate being (in Greek *mesitēs* or "mediator"), a function demanded by many religions of Apuleius' times—as much by the pagan religions, such as the Mithras cult, as by Christianity. For Christians, Christ

48. The Greek *daimōn* (in Latin, *daemon*) is of course employed here as a technical term; it did not mean simply "demon" or "evil spirit."

functioned as the intermediary between the God of the Old Testament and the men to whom the New Testament was addressed: "For there is one God, and one mediator (*mesitēs*) between God and men, the man Christ Jesus; who gave himself a ransom for all, to be testified in due time" (I *Timothy* 2:5–6).

Within the realm of the *daimones* various levels of power exist. A *propheta*, such as Zatchlas in Book 2, may be like ordinary men, but Cupid approaches the status of divinity:

Moreover, there are certain divine powers of a middle kind, placed in this interspace of the air, between the highest ether and the earth far below, through whom both our desires and our deserts pass on the way to the gods. These the Greeks call by the name of *daimones*. Messengers between the inhabitants of earth and of heaven, they carry from one to the other prayers and gifts, supplications and assistance; they are interpreters and bearers of greetings for both. Through these same demons, as Plato affirms in his *Symposium*, are directed all revelations, the various miracles of magicians, and all kinds of predictions. [*On the God of Socrates* 6]

Whether it is Cupid intervening to save Psyche in the pretty fable of Books 4 to 6 or the genuinely religious experience of Isis' appearance to Lucius in Book 11, the presence of these intermediate creatures is required to connect the perfect world of the gods with the imperfect world of human beings:

There is, however, another class of *daimones*, not fewer in number, far and away more excelling in their dignity, superior and august, who are forever liberated from the bonds and bounds of the body, and who have certain powers in their charge. Of this number are Sleep [Somnus] and Love [Amor]. They have different powers: Love rouses to consciousness, Sleep lulls to rest. [*On the God of Socrates* 16]

Following Plato (e.g., *Phaedo* 107D, *Timaeus* 90A, *Republic* 10.617D–619A), Apuleius explains that a *daimōn* of such importance as Amor oversees an individual's life and supervises its way through the world. At the end of a life, the *daimōn* calls the *psyche* to account for its actions. Since Diotima told Socrates that human nature could not easily find a better helper (*synergos*) to attain immortality than Eros (*Symposium* 212B), Psyche would seem to be unusually fortunate in her *daimōn*. In fact, her path to immortality is not to be an easy one.

The Fall of Psyche

The elaborate series of explicit warnings that Cupid gives his wife in Book 5 resembles the rather subtler ones that crossed Lucius' path in Books 1–3. This part of the tale is a clear indication that we are going back over some of the same ground we covered in those earlier books, but at a more abstract and allegorical level. The basic difference is that whereas it was magic and all its dangers that the impetuous Lucius wished to learn, something far less sinister and harmful is involved here. How could the god of love—usually named Cupid in this tale but sometimes named Amor—pose any threat to his own wife?[49] Why the secrecy of his marriage bed? In part the allegory demands it: Lucius' "initiation" into magic in Book 3 involved learning and seeing things he should not have learned and seen; and by Book 11 he will have learned to keep from revealing the secrets of the Isis cult to the "curious reader." But the main reason Cupid is right in refusing to reveal his identity to Psyche and that Psyche is wrong to insist on seeing him lies in the nature of Cupid himself. Of his nature Apuleius says elsewhere: "There are also intermediate forces of the gods, *powers that one is allowed to sense but which are not given to us to see,* such as the class of Love and other gods: *their form is unseen, their force is perceived*" ("'sunt et aliae mediae deum potestates, quas licet sentire, non datur cernere, ut Amoris ceterorumque id genus, quorum forma invisitata, vis cognita") (*Florida* 10). When Psyche sees her husband at last and injures him, she violates the secret identity of the god. Although we cannot trace a direct connection between any ancient artistic monument and the events of Apuleius' novel,[50] a certain antagonism is often apparent between Cupid and Psyche. They are not always embracing; some-

49. For an explanation of the distinctions between the Latin names Amor and Cupido, see Antonie Wlosok, "Amor and Cupido," *Harvard Studies in Classical Philology* 79 (1975), 165–179.

50. See Carl C. Schlam, *Cupid and Psyche: Apuleius and the Monuments* (University Park, Pa., 1976), 31–40.

times she is shown advancing upon the sleeping god, and sometimes she is depicted applying a torch to his body.

The symbolic meaning of Apuleius' allegory should, then, be plain enough. When through her curiosity Psyche discovers what it was not meant for her to know—Cupid's identity—she loses that *daimōn* who has the power or *potestas* to bind her with the immortal gods. This is the meaning of the sequel to her discovery of Cupid's identity: it is, literally, the fall of the soul (cf. Plato, *Phaedrus* 248C–D). She attempts to hold on to Cupid, but cannot and falls backward to earth (5.24). Psyche, who attempts to posesss Cupid, is *qua* human imperfect, but she will earn a reprieve. By divine grace she may be rescued from Venus, just as Lucius may be rescued somehow from Fortuna caeca, blind Fortune.

6. Psyche applying torch to Cupid. Palazzo Corsetti, Rome. Reproduced by permission of the Deutsches Archäologisches Institut, Rome.

Erich Neumann's psychoanalytical interpretation of the Cupid and Psyche story is well enough known to deserve comment at this point. His thesis is that the tale may be read as an allegorical account of the development of the feminine psyche: "It is the awakening of Psyche as the psyche, the fateful moment in the life of the feminine, in which for the first time the woman emerges from the darkness of her unconscious and the harshness of her matriarchal captivity and, in individual encounters with the masculine, loves, that is recognizes, Eros."[51] Apuleius' own words in *On the God of Socrates*, no less than the need for a *mesitēs* expressed by the religions of his day, show that Neumann's reading strays too far from the essential meaning of the tale. Indeed, Apuleius' point is much simpler. In terms of theology, Book 5 shows how man and god may be separated. Book 6 will show how they may be rejoined.

BOOK 6

Psyche, abandoned by her husband, appeals to Ceres (2–3) and Juno (4) for aid and for refuge from Venus. Like proper Roman matrons, both goddesses turn her away; it is not permitted to harbor fugitive slaves. Finally Psyche surrenders herself to Venus (8–9). After being scourged at the hands of Venus' servants, she is compelled to undertake a series of three labors: sorting out a mixed pile of grain and seed (10), cropping wool from a flock of rams (12), and capturing water from the river Styx in a phial (13–15). With the miraculous aid of ants, a kindly reed growing by the flock of rams, and an eagle sent down by Jove to catch the waters of the Styx, Psyche accomplishes all three tasks. Venus then sets her the last and most difficult labor: to descend to Hades and bring back from Proserpina a jar containing divine beauty (16). Psyche despairs at the impossibility

51. Erich Neumann, *Amor and Psyche: The Psychic Development of the Feminine,* trans. Ralph Manheim, Bollingen Series 54 (Princeton, N.J., 1956), 77–78. Neumann is of course not concerned with a literary interpretation of Apuleius. For a good introduction to the psychoanalytical school, see Anthony Starr, *C. G. Jung* (New York, 1973).

of this task and is at the point of hurling herself from the tower when the tower is suddenly given voice and advises her in great detail as to how this journey may be accomplished (17–19). She then passes swiftly through all the terrors of the underworld without coming to harm (20); as soon as she sees the light of day, however, she is overcome by curiosity to see what is in Proserpina's jar (20–21). No sooner does she open the jar than she is overwhelmed by a deathlike sleep, from which only Cupid's intervention saves her (21). Cupid then appeals to Jove to free Psyche from Venus' wrath, and the request is granted (22). Psyche is made immortal (23), and all the gods, including Venus, celebrate her wedding. After a time a child named Voluptas, or Pleasure, is born to Cupid and Psyche (24).

So ends the old woman's story of consolation. It appears to have little bearing on the fate of either Lucius or the young maiden, for when they attempt to escape they are easily recaptured by the bandits (27–30). The book ends with a speech by one of their captors, enthusiastically describing the tortures that await the pair on the morrow (31–32).

Psyche Fails Again

When Ceres and Juno reluctantly deny refuge to Psyche, she is thrown on the mercy of her bitterest enemy, Venus—now synonymous with Fortune.[52] Although the tale still is of some interest to the disconsolate young maiden sitting in the robbers' cave, it is to Lucius' own situation that Psyche's trials now come to seem more than ever relevant. The first two labors of Psyche are bridal tests set for her by a wicked stepmother; the last two, involving contact with the world of the dead, are reminiscent of the rites of such a chthonic cult as that of Demeter and Kore at Eleusis.[53] Here in Book 6 comes one test after another of Psyche; she is a kind of initiate, but an initiate into what? The cruelty of Venus is nicely balanced by a series of helpful friends. The tower

52. The prayers of Psyche at 6.2 and 6.4 resemble the prayer of Lucius at 11.2, still one other parallel between her trials and those of Lucius. Both seek the "hope of salvation" (*spes salutis*; cf. 6.5 with 11.1).
53. See George E. Mylonas, *Eleusis and the Eleusinian Mysteries* (Princeton, N.J., 1969), 15.

that so helpfully and precisely instructs Psyche about her journey through the underworld describes the sort of secrets that Lucius later feels constrained to guard from the profane and curious (cf. 6.18–19 with 11.23). But Psyche's visit to Prosperina is actually described before it happens, through the speech of the tower, and we hear nothing here in Book 6 that we could not find elsewhere in other Greek or Roman descriptions of the underworld; for instance, Aristophanes' *Frogs* or Book 6 of the *Aeneid*. (Only in Book 11 will we find a mission to the underworld, which, like Odysseus' visit with the shades in *Odyssey* 11 or Aeneas's journey with the Sibyl in *Aeneid* 6, is truly one of purpose accomplished; and then, true to form, Apuleius will refrain for reasons of piety from telling his readers any of the details of Lucius' peregrinations in the underworld.)

When Psyche returns to the light of the upper world with her tasks accomplished, her salvation seems assured. But then for the second time she indulges her inveterate curiosity by opening the jar (*pyxis*) of Proserpina in the hope of discovering the divine beauty said to be inside. Her fate is the same as Lucius' in Book 3 (cf. Fotis' *pyxis* at 3.24 with Proserpina's at 6.20–21). In their eagerness to discover some kind of transcendental power, both are very nearly destroyed by an evil force. But both are entirely innocent, and it is this innocence or guilelessness (*simplicitas*) that is the chief virtue of Psyche, Lucius, and even Apuleius himself (cf. 5.18, 5.24, 11.16, and *Apology* 43).

Pandora's box has been opened once again, though in a different setting, and evil is again let loose on the world. Yet this newest disaster is also the occasion for hope. We must remember that when Pandora opened her box and let loose so many evils on the world, Hope (Elpis) was caught at the lid and captured (see Hesiod's version of the story in *Works and Days* 42–105). Hope is the ironic consolation that makes mortals believe their misfortunes may be endured and overcome.[54] In this instance the cause for hope is that Psyche's second failure inspires Cupid's return.

With Psyche's failure and Cupid's rescue of her we have

54. For later artistic transformations of this scene, see Dora and Erwin Panofsky, *Pandora's Box: The Changing Aspects of a Mythical Symbol* (New York, 1956).

reached the climax of the tale and the focal scene of the novel. At the most abstract level, the allegory at this point conveys an idea basic to our understanding of the human condition. For purposes of clarity, let us translate the names of our two characters into their English equivalents, that is, Psyche = Soul, Cupid = Love.

Love's reappearance at 6.22 signifies that Soul cannot survive save by divine intervention. Never before in the novel has Soul's vulnerability in the face of Fortune been so clearly revealed. However hard Soul may strive to work out its own salvation—and we must remember that the tales of both Psyche and Lucius ultimately represent that struggle—it evidently cannot do so unaided. Some divine power must intervene if Soul is to be saved—not only from Fortune's buffeting but from itself as well. The tale has shown that curiosity is an integral part of Soul; it has shown also that Soul veers toward its own destruction if left to itself. The necessity of intervention by a *daimōn* such as Love is therefore beyond doubt. We must remember that Socrates worshiped his guiding *daimōn* as though it were itself a god (*On the God of Socrates* 17).

Thus Psyche's failure in her last ordeal reveals a powerful justification for choosing the religious life, as Lucius will elect to do in Book 11. The final scenes of the tale—Soul's fall, Love's intervention, and the benign favor of the supreme god (Jupiter), who grants Love his wish—occupy the cardinal points of Apuleius' eleven books of metamorphoses.

With Psyche's entrance into the company of the Olympian gods, a bond is established between Soul and god through the agency of Love, and Soul is then admitted to what Plato urged was the highest goal it could attain—knowledge of the divine (*Symposium* 210E). Through the birth of a child named Voluptas (Pleasure, or perhaps Joy), we infer that true happiness cannot come into being until such time as Soul acquires knowledge of the divine. Diotima's last words to Socrates make much the same point:

"What, then, do we think would occur," she said, "if it happened that one could gaze on beauty itself, unalloyed, pure, and unmixed, not infected with the flesh and color of humanity and so much more of mortal nonsense? What if one could gaze on divine beauty itself, in its single form? Do you think it would be a sorry life for a man to look there, to observe that sight properly and have it be with him? Or do you not consider," she said, "that only he who sees through that which makes it visible will be given to breed not illusions of virtue but true examples of virtue, inasmuch as he reaches not for an illusion but for the truth? For the one who has begotten true virtue and nurtured it will be called beloved of god; and if ever any man is immortal, he is, of all men." [Plato, *Symposium* 211E–212A]

In the light of such a doctrine we can appreciate Lucius' desire to escape enslavement to blind Fortune and embrace the provident Fortune of Book 11. His conversion to Isis, like the tale of Cupid and Psyche, reflects Apuleius' sense of the precariousness of the human condition and the necessary terms for our happiness. At first there seems much cause for hope in the tale of Cupid and Psyche.

Spiritual Serenity and the Surrounding World

As was observed earlier, nothing is more understandable than the temptation to treat Cupid and Psyche's tale as something distinct from the rest of the novel. If the reader can resist that temptation, however, it must be realized that it would be equally misguided to take the tale for some kind of blueprint that can explain every aspect of Lucius' story. Book 6 is not merely an adaptation of Platonic doctrine into fiction, nor is it a simple rehearsal in allegorical terms for what Lucius will experience in Book 11; for it does not in fact end with the lovely, encouraging scene of the birth of Voluptas. Apuleius has instead contrived a remarkable dissonance that will be resolved only by Lucius' conversion in Book 11.[55] A tale that seems to offer an ecstatic, supernatural release from mortality is followed by a less pleasant turn of events for the maiden Charite and Lucius. Well may Lucius regret not having had a tablet and stylus to take it down (6.25). Charite and Lucius elude the old woman only to be caught trying to escape. Just before they fall back into the

55. Contrast in the tone of the novel has been noted in Walsh, *Roman Novel*, 182, and Gilbert Highet, *The Anatomy of Satire* (Princeton, N.J., 1962), 182, though not with specific reference to Book 6.

clutches of the bandits, Charite is quite overcome by what she believes to be her deliverance from Fortune. Her speech is replete with mythological allusions and useless promises of honor to be bestowed on the animal that carries her—as if to emphasize her self-delusion in rejoicing over her good fortune. The scene is not without its ridiculous aspect.[56] What follows deserves our closest attention.

When Charite and Lucius are recaptured and returned to the camp, they see the old woman who had told the tale of Cupid and Psyche hanging from a tree. She has killed herself rather than risk the robbers' displeasure. Her body is thrown over the cliff and the bandits sit down to eat the hot meal she prepared. Various punishments are then proposed for Lucius and Charite, but the one that most captures the bandits' fancy is described in as bizarre a passage as any that appears in *The Golden Ass*. An anonymous bandit proposes that the ass be slain and that his guts be scooped out and replaced by the naked maiden. Sewn up inside, she is to be left to perish amid the stench and maggots of the rotting carcass. The torture is described in fastidious, loving detail, and it is on this note that Book 6 ends.

Ancient novelists reveled in this kind of Grand Guignol. In Xenophon of Ephesus, pirates debate a variety of equally ingenious punishments for the captive maiden Anthia (4.6);[57] a comparable episode in Achilles Tatius' *Clitophon and Leucippe* (3.15–17) describes the apparent disembowelment and cannibalistic sacrifice of the heroine, and the same speech appears in a parallel scene of *Lucius or the Ass* (25–26). But no Greek novelist appears to have created quite the kind of contrast we may observe in Book 6 of *The Golden Ass*, between the pretty allegory of Cupid and Psyche and the imminent butchery of Lucius and Charite.

A longing to flee this world's evils may sooner or later be any person's experience, of course; it is no discovery on the part of Apuleius. But there is a particular artistry in the way he treats

56. Charite sees her ride on the ass as a chance to achieve the glory of the mythological rides of Arion on a dolphin and Europa on Jove disguised as a bull (6.29); only those rides were successful for at least one of the pair involved.
57. Walsh, *Roman Novel*, 159 and note.

this familiar theme. As we shall see in Chapter 4, whatever his credentials as a philosopher, there is little question that he was very familiar with Plato on at least the literary level, and that is a useful point to keep in mind when we read Book 6. Frequently Socrates must squarely face the difficulty inherent in choosing the life of the philosopher while remaining in a mundane and often hostile world; see the *Apology passim,* and especially *Gorgias* 482C–486D and *Republic* 1.336B–344B, where he wrestles with Callicles and Thrasymachus, two resourceful opponents of the philosophical life. Socrates' life and teaching remind us that a philosopher may construct his image of an ideal state or of the divine, but that he does so in a world that constantly impinges on that image and threatens to destroy it.

A similarly jarring contrast may be caught in such a popular philosophy as the Stoicism of Marcus Aurelius, one of the emperors contemporary with Apuleius. Marcus treated philosophy as a religion, as did Apuleius, and found in it a consolation and a bulwark against the tribulations of the world. A typical statement of Marcus' esteem for philosophy may be found in his *Meditations* 2.17. The calm resignation of the philosopher-emperor is apparent in the relief sculptures of the Marcus Aurelius Column in Rome (see Figures 7, 8, and 9), commemorating his wars on the northern frontier of the empire in the early 170s.[58] The artists who executed this monument have juxtaposed scenes of philosophical and imperial serenity with vivid episodes of cruelty and suffering. The ensemble conveys the ennobling idea that here is a leader who can be near to the horrors of war and yet, almost like some Olympian god on a Greek temple frieze, remote from them.[59]

Similarly, the juxtaposition of exaltation and cruelty in Book 6: how can we reconcile the lovely vision of the Cupid and Psyche myth with the gruesome notions with which the book actually ends? Are we meant to reconcile them? The narrator of the tale is now dead—first swinging from a tree, then thrown over a

---

58. See Anthony Birley, *Marcus Aurelius* (London, 1966), and P. G. Hamberg, *Studies in Roman Imperial Art* (Uppsala and Copenhagen, 1945).

59. For an early (and more restrained) exaltation of an emperor, see Vergil's description of Augustus at the battle of Actium, *Aeneid* 8.678–681.

7. Marcus Aurelius and lieutenants. Relief sculpture on the Marcus Aurelius Column, Rome. Reproduced by permission of the Deutsches Archäologisches Institut, Rome.

8. Execution of prisoners. Relief sculpture on the Marcus Aurelius Column, Rome. Reproduced by permission of the Deutsches Archäologisches Institut, Rome.

9. Parade of prisoners before Marcus Aurelius. Relief sculpture on the Marcus Aurelius Column, Rome. Reproduced by permission of the Deutsches Archäologisches Institut, Rome.

cliff—as if to underscore the unreality of her charming tale. In this simple way Book 6 creates a tension between the absurdities and cruelties of this world and a longing for a paradisic release from them that will intensify with every succeeding book of Lucius' story.

BOOK 7

The next morning a bandit appears to report that the robbery of Milo's house has been blamed on Lucius, the young guest who disappeared at the time of the crime (1–2). This new occasions a grand outburst from the ass about the unfair ways of blind Fortune (2–3). A new recruit then arrives and quickly wins the bandits' hearts by his tales of daring and bravery (4–5). The most notable of the many adventures he relates is the tale of Plotina, a virtuous wife who saved her husband by her courage and by disguising herself as a man (6–8). The bandits miss the hint. This new robber, called Haemus, is in fact Tlepolemus, husband of the maiden whose name is here at last revealed to be Charite (12). Tlepolemus soon has the entire band of robbers sodden with wine, then drugged to sleep. The young couple and Lucius make their escape to the town, return with their friends, and dispatch the bandits at their leisure (13). Lucius thinks he is to be rewarded for his part in the adventure by being put out to pasture (15), but capricious Fortune delivers him instead to a cruel woman who makes him work all day at a mill (16–18). He also suffers beatings and pranks at the hands of an evil boy who uses him as a pack animal; the boy falsely complains of the ass's sexual assaults on boys and women (19–23). Lucius is then miraculously saved by a huge bear (not of Thrasyleon's kind), which devours the lad (24). When the boy's mother tries to punish Lucius by thrusting a torch between his hind legs, he escapes by a timely diarrhetic discharge in the woman's face (27–28).

The Bandits Become a Joke

From this point until the end of Book 10, Lucius passes through a bewildering series of reversals of fortune as time and again he or others wrongly anticipate the course of events. Appropriate enough, then, are his bitter complaints about blind Fortune, the cause of all his troubles. He realizes ruefully that the former state of the human Lucius was indeed enviable, and he may well regret his earlier lighthearted remarks about accepting whatever Fortune decrees (cf. 1.20 with 7.2–3). But recognizing the fickle ways of Dame Fortune is only the beginning of his woes, for he is about to enter more deeply than ever into the world of Fortuna caeca, blind fortune, from which only seeing Fortune, Isis videns, will be able to save him.

The name of the unfortunate maiden is at last revealed to be Charite—a single Grace, as it were, stepping out from the traditional trio of Graces. The central books of *The Golden Ass* thereby comes into focus as an elaborate panel of the complementary tales of one Grace and Cupid and Psyche. The three Graces, Cupids, and Psyches can often be found together in ancient monuments. It is as if the sarcophagus relief in Figure 10, showing Graces flanked by Cupids and Psyches, had been adapted to a literary setting. In Books 4–8 of *The Golden Ass*, the tableau is reversed: Charite and Tlepolemus frame Cupid and Psyche. This is not the only point in the novel where we may trace some connection between Apuleius' tales and the visual arts.[60]

Tlepolemus, the brave young husband of Charite, appears and contrives an easy rescue from the perilous situation Lucius and Charite faced at the end of Book 6. He plays on the well-established improvidence of the bandits, lulling their suspicions by the heroic and bombastic story of the virtuous wife Plotina. He compounds the masquerade with a story about exploits in the dress of a woman. His speech is doubly ironic, for it conceals not only the private joke he and Charite enjoy in deceiving the robbers but, as is the rule in this novel, a foreshadowing of their own unhappy future. Like the fictive Plotina, Charite will be compelled to assume a man's role to avenge her husband.

For the moment, though, all seems well. "Haemus'" plan works perfectly, and the menacing thugs of Book 6 are all dis-

---

60. In addition to the description of the sculpture at 2.4, see the account of the sleeping Cupid at 5.22 and my discussion of that passage in Chapter 5.

10. A trio of *Charites*, or Graces, flanked by Cupids and Psyches. Sarcophagous relief sculpture, Palazzo Mattei, Rome. Reproduced by permission of the Deutsches Archäologisches Institut, Rome.

posed of by wine. The trick is as old a literary device as the one Odysseus thought up to get out of Polyphemus' cave. Soon, however, what seemed like deliverance turns into a nightmare, and in 7.28 Lucius nearly suffers the fate of Meleager, whose mother extinguished his life by burning up his "life-token," a torch. This part of the story is an elegant mixture of myth and scatology, nor is it the only such instance.

Lucius frequently makes such rueful mythological allusions. In addition to the reference to Meleager near the end of Book 7, his tormentor, the evil boy, is referred to as "my very Bellerophon" (7.26), the bandits are like the Lapiths and the Centaurs (4.8), the old woman who attempts to restrain Lucius is a "Dirce hanging from an ass" (6.27), only Harpies could eat as much as Lucius consumed and get away with it (10.15), and Lucius flees as swiftly as Pegasus (8.16). His own odyssey is sprinkled with ingenious twists to classical myth. Among the most bizarre is 7.28: whatever Meleager's mother may have done with her torch, the one thing it could *not* have been was what the dead boy's mother seeks to do to Lucius.

BOOK 8

Lucius now hears the dismaying news of the death of Charite and Tlepolemus (1). A servant tells the story: Thrasyllus fell in love with Charite and treacherously murdered his friend Tlepolemus in a boar hunt to win her for himself (2–14). When Thrasyllus pressed his suit with the young widow, she rejected him in horror (18). That night the ghost of her murdered husband appeared to the grieving wife, telling of his death at the hand of his best friend (8–9). Feigning acceptance of Thrasyllus' advances (9), Charite drugged his wine and took her revenge by scratching out his eyes with a hairpin (10–12). She committed suicide at the tomb of her husband and was buried at his side by loyal servants (13–14). Thrasyllus then starved himself to death within the tomb in expiation of his sins (14).

Overcome with the horror of this tale, the surviving members of the household flee into the country (15), undergoing a series of terrible experiences on the way. Lucius finally is sold to a new master, Philebus, one of a band of depraved priests of the Dea Syria, or Atargatis (25–26). As pack animal for the priests he witnesses both their masochistic rites and their debauching of a rustic youth. When the priests are discovered *in flagrante* (29), they flee to another town. At the very end of the book the wife of the cook of his latest host proposes that Lucius be butchered to replace a piece of venison eaten by a dog (31).

Romantic Love Becomes a Joke

Book 8 opens with a servant's report of the death of grace itself as embodied in the maiden Charite. She and her young husband had enjoyed the kind of happy consummation of their love that can be found in many an ancient Greek novel.[61] But once again Apuleius carries us beyond our expectations into a disorienting and disoriented world. True to the novel's theme of rapid and unexpected transformations, Charite is changed by the murder of her husband into a fury who scratches out Thrasyllus' eyes with a hairpin. Her long speech (8.12) reveals the same taste for feverish rhetoric as does Book 6 (28–29), only in this instance Charite—now as misnamed as Socrates in Book 1—carries out her intentions. By disposing so brutally of the one idealized, sentimental pair of lovers in the whole novel, Apuleius parts company with the somewhat gentler conventions of the Greek novelists. Not infrequently other characters of those authors may come to grief; but the general rule is for the protagonists to reach the end of their journey together—and intact.

Lucius has by now witnessed one stunning reversal after another in people's fortunes. In the course of Books 4–8 Charite seemed at first lost, was then miraculously saved, and is now at last destroyed by Fortune. The adulterer Thrasyllus is a classic type, a person in the grip of base desires. Abandoned to the pleasures of the senses, he goes mad with lust for Charite, and although unable to conquer her virtue, he effectively destroys

61. For the typical plot of a Greek romance, see Chapter 3. A wife's devotion to her husband even to the death is one of the oldest themes in Greek fiction; see the novella of Panthea and Abradatas interspersed through three books of Xenophon's *Education of Cyrus* (5.1, 6.1, and especially 7.3).

her through his murder of Tlepolemus. True to his name (formed from the Greek *thrasus*, meaning "rash" or "hasty"), he slays his handsome and too trusting young friend on a boar hunt. It is a crime resembling the story of Atys and Adrastus as told in Herodotus (1.34–45). As for Charite, she has the unhappy duty of playing in real life the role of the brave Plotina, heroine of Haemus-Tlepolemus' story (cf. 7.6–8 with 8.8–15).

Fortune is now complete master of Lucius' world. As the members of Charite's household flee the scene of tragedy, they pass through an inferno of suffering and supernatural events in the face of which they are almost entirely helpless. The path of their journey is marked by one disaster after another. Every page of Book 8 reeks of death. Thus, a villager who speaks to the travelers is perched in a cypress tree (8.18); we might recall a similarly dire moment in the Cupid and Psyche tale (5.24). In both instances, the cypress is a symbol of death.[62] During this journey, Lucius recounts a strange, horrid little episode about the adultery of a steward, his wife's revenge, and the punishment the steward's master meted out: the poor wretch was tied to a tree, smeared with honey, and eaten alive by ants (8.22). Three basic themes—adultery, revenge, and death—are announced here, as leitmotifs. The reader will observe the elaboration of these themes in the next two books of the novel.

Deliverance for Lucius, such as it is, comes when he is sold to Philebus ("Boy lover"). The girls (*puellae*, 8.26) of the Dea Syria unfortunately prove to be cruel masters. Their particular mixture of avarice, masochism, and sodomy is a grotesque reverse image of the life Lucius will eventually lead as a *pastophor* of Isis in Book 11.[63]

BOOK 9

Lucius is saved from the cook's knife by the news of an outbreak of hydrophobia infecting the animals of the house (1–2).

62. Franz Cumont, *Recherches sur le symbolisme funéraire des Romains* (Paris, 1942), 219.
63. A *pastophor* was a priest who earned alms by carrying around the image of a deity in a portable shrine.

He is isolated for a time, but when it is clear he is free from the infection, his life with the priests of the Dea Syria resumes its course (3). He recounts the story of a poor man cuckolded by his wife (the tale of the tub [5–7]). Soon afterward the priests are apprehended for their theft of a golden goblet from the altar of the Mother of the Gods (Cybele), and Lucius acquires a baker as his new master (8–10). He then tells three complicated stories of adultery: the tale of the young lover Philesitherus and his cuck-olding of Barbarus; the tale of the fuller's wife, in which an adulterer chokes in a sulfur basket used for bleaching; and the tale of the baker's wife, in which his master, the baker, is mur-dered by black magic after discovering his wife's adultery with the young Philesitherus (14–31). Lucius is then sold to a poor gardener, whose extreme poverty causes both of them much suffering (32). He recounts the tale of the cruel landlord, in which three brothers are slain for defending their rights; when the father hears the story, he cuts his throat in his grief (33–38). The gardener runs afoul of a cruel Roman soldier (39), and Lucius' irrepressible curiosity eventually betrays his master to the authorities (42). This soldier becomes Lucius' next master.

Tales of Adultery: Experience Never Teaches

Books 9 and 10 are filled with an elaborate series of tales with similar plots and dissimilar endings. A tradition existed in an-tiquity, beginning with Semonides in the mid-seventh century B.C., of cataloguing the vices of women. In Latin literature the longest example of this kind of dispraise is Juvenal, *Satires* 6 (written ca. A.D. 116). The tale of the widow of Ephesus in Petro-nius' *Satyricon* (111–112) is very similar in spirit to the tales of Book 9, and of particular interest to readers of Apuleius, since Lucius recounts not one story of this kind but six. As with the tales of Aristomenes and Thelyphron, there is potentially as much danger for those telling or listening to these stories as for the characters within them. The tales are not mere variations on a theme; they are repeated for a purpose.

The cumulative effect of the adultery stories is to satiate the reader with the theme. At first we may be amused to hear about men and women who let lust rule their lives, but each successive tale arouses alternately false and true expectations. The complicated tale-within-a-tale concerning Philesitherus and Barbarus is a tour de force, as Lucius himself has promised it will be (9.14).[64] It ends with the husband hanged by magic and his daughter lamenting the ruin of her family. This is an unexpected finish to Book 9's cheerful stories of gossip and adultery—as if *The Marriage of Figaro* ended with the poisoning of Count Almaviva.

Book 9 leaves us suspended amid a bewildering range of contradictory feelings: Is adultery merely funny, as it is, for example, in Petronius? Or is it tragic, as in the outcome of the tale of Barbarus and his wife? The cleverness of the wife in the tale of the tub is purest Milesian ribaldry, yet the following story of Barbarus' Christian wife provides a frighteningly gloomy twist to what is essentially the same theme—the easy deception of a gullible husband.[65] By repeating the motif in such closely juxtaposed stories, Apuleius forcefully conveys an impression of life ruled by Fortune's laws. If we can recall the brief tale in Book 8 about the steward and his wife (8.22), we now realize that it is an overture to the predominant themes of the tales in Books 9 and 10.

For anyone who wants to know everything or as much as possible (1.2), there is an advantage to being encased in an animal's body. As Lucius boasts, he is now privileged to enjoy an Odyssean view of the world (9.13). Because of his disguised form, everyone he meets goes about his ordinary business, however murderous or foolish that business may be, and Lucius is able to see human character frankly revealed. A likely inspiration for Lucius' ideas about his ideal vantage point for observing the human condition is the second half of the *Odyssey*, where Athena disguises Odysseus as a filthy beggar:

64. Like the tale of the tub (9.5-7), this story (9.14-31) was ingeniously revised by Boccaccio and appears in his *Decameron* (Fifth Day, Tale 10, concerning Pietro di Vinciolo and his wife).

65. The wife worships one God, "whom she declared to be the only one" (9.14). The Romans found the fanatical monotheism of the early Christians quite unreasonable; see Tacitus' account of the Christians and the burning of Rome in *Annals* 15.44 and especially the letter from Pliny the Younger to Trajan about his interrogation of recalcitrant Christians in the province of Bithynia, ca. A.D. 110 (*Letters* 10.96).

Come then, I shall render you unknown to all mortals, I shall shrivel the fair skin on your supple limbs, I shall destroy the flaxen hair on your head. I shall wrap you in such a garment that any man would shudder to see it, I shall dim your eyes that were before so fair, so that you might seem mean to all the suitors and to your wife and son, whom you left behind in your halls. [*Odyssey*, 13.397–403]

The picture of humanity revealed to Odysseus is just as discouraging as that seen in *The Golden Ass*. The weak and the helpless, including domestic animals, represent an invitation to the unwary to reveal their true characters. The theme of the unrecognized or even unseen observer is also popular in later Greek literature.[66] Odysseus' disguise exposes the baseness of Penelope's suitors and the treachery of certain members of his household; similarly, Lucius' improbable form enables him to see the good or bad in each person he meets. In other respects the two have little in common. Odysseus executed the suitors and set his house in order. Lucius, instead of mastering the world about him, is approaching an experience that will remove him from that world altogether. In this sense, his odyssey is a mockery of the original *Odyssey*, and he himself is a mockery of that poem's hero.

BOOK 10

Lucius hears the tale of the wicked stepmother and recounts it for his listeners' benefit (2–12). He introduces it portentously as grand tragedy, in the style of Phaedra and Hippolytus (2). Yet because of the providence of a wise and kindly doctor, the poison used by the wicked stepmother does not kill the older boy's half brother; the poison was only a harmless sleeping potion (11). Lucius is then sold to two brothers, a pastry cook and an expert roaster of meats (13). He begins to live a life of luxury,

---

66. For a similar acid test of human nature, cf. the story of Gyges' ring in Plato, *Republic* 2.359D–360A. Turned a certain way, the ring made Gyges invisible; he could then watch other people without their being able to see him. The same tale (without the ring) also appears in Herodotus 1.8–13.

relishing the choice foods cooked by his new masters (14–15). His human tastes are soon discovered, and he becomes such a novelty that he is sold by the brothers to their master, Thiasus, who becomes the last of Lucius' masters (16). A series of public banquets and performances is held in which Lucius is the star. He delights everyone with his uncanny ability to understand human spech and enjoy human society. He is careful, though, not to reveal how completely human his intelligence is, lest he be taken for a magician (17–18). He then sleeps with a matron who becomes infatuated with his miraculous talents (19–22). The euphoria is shattered when Lucius learns that he is to be made to copulate with a condemned murderess in the arena at Corinth. Both of them will then be devoured by wild beasts. The last of the tales in Book 10 concerns this woman, who mistakenly sees her chaste sister-in-law as an adulteress (23–28). With the aid of an absent-minded doctor, she murders five people, including the doctor and her own daughter (28). Moments before Lucius is to be led out to her, he witnesses a pantomime of the judgment of Paris, a scene he interprets as the inevitable triumph of injustice in human affairs (30–32). Terrified at the prospect of being torn apart by some wild beast and disgusted at the prospect of lying down with the convicted murderess, Lucius bolts out of the arena and heads for nearby Cenchreae. Soon he is fast asleep (35).

The Providence of Two Doctors and Two Evil Wives

The two brothers and their master, Thiasus (*thiasos* is Greek for "revel"), treat Lucius as if he were a human being, and ironically, in Book 10 he is human in everything but form. The revelry of the banquet hall and the pleasures of the kindly matron's bed seem to be rewards for his earlier suffering.[67] Yet Book 10 reinforces the contrast between these pleasures of the flesh and the increasingly savage cast of characters that populate the last two tales of *The Golden Ass*. Here the human comedy turns

67. The copulation of a woman and an ass—a crude enough subject—is crudely represented on several lamps and other artifacts from Greek antiquity; see Philippe Bruneau, "Illustrations Antiques du *Coq* et de l'*Ane* de Lucien," *Bulletin de Correspondence Hellenique* 89 (1965), 349–357, Figs. 4–6.

increasingly from the ribaldry of the tale of the tub toward melodrama and tragedy. Apuleius' wicked wives and stepmothers resemble the kinds of women Juvenal describes toward the end of his long satire on women (*Satires* 6.627–661). As in Book 9, the two tales with their happy and unhappy endings reveal Fortune's unpredictable ways. The first tale, resembling the story of Phaedra and Hippolytus, is given a florid introduction, as if we were about to hear a tragedy: "iam ergo, lector optime, scito te tragoediam, non fabulum legere et a socco ad coturnum ascendere" ("'Now, excellent reader, know that you are to read not a tale but a tragedy, and that you ascend from the comic boot to the tragic buskin") (10.2). A tragedy the tale may be, yet the "divine providence" of a doctor rescues the stepson from his wicked stepmother. Apuleius is not confused or irresolute here, nor is it plausible that he did not know how this tale was going to turn out.[68] On the contrary, this solemn introduction is for the reader's benefit. It deliberately misleads us, so that, as everywhere else in the novel, we are totally confounded in our expectations. It remains for the second tale, with its unnamed woman (*vilis aliqua*, "a certain base woman"), to bring about real tragedy. Juvenal had described this type and had employed the same *topos*, or rhetorical commonplace, of ascending to the *cothurnus* of tragedy:

> fingimus haec altum satura sumente cothurnum
> scilicet, et finem egressi legemque priorum
> grande Sophocleo carmen bacchamur hiatu,
> montibus ignotum Rutulis caeloque Latino?
> nos utinam vani.

> To fashion these tales do you think our satire takes up the lofty buskin of tragedy? Have we stepped over the law and limit of our predecessors to revel in a song of Sophoclean tone, with a theme unknown to the Rutulian hills and the Latin sky? Would that ours were an idle tale! [Juvenal, *Satires* 6.634–638]

---

68. Cf. Walsh, *Roman Novel*, 171: "Our author seems hardly to have known how his story was going to end, and this gives us the clearest picture of the rapidity with which he assembles different stories into an uneasy unity." There is a similar plot in the story of Asclepiades; see the translation of *Florida* 19 in Appendix 1.

The *vilis aliqua* of Book 10 is as fiendish as any described by Juvenal. She completes the gallery of witches, old women, and adulterous wives that has been on display since the tale of Aristomenes in Book 1. She is a type rather popular in Latin love elegy and satire.[69] Now she is about to step out into the arena at Corinth. Of all the punishments that could have been devised for her, the one hit upon is perhaps the most shocking: Lucius is to be her punishment. The horror of it is that his voluptuous world and the "entertaining" world of the Milesian tale are in this way combined.

As for human *providentia*, the helplessness of the doctor in the second tale serves to underscore the limitations of human understanding. The doctor in the first tale averted one tragedy, but this second doctor cannot even save himself. Once again Apuleius has used two like characters to make a point; compare this observation about the doctors with my earlier analysis of the contrast between Diophanes and Zatchlas in Book 2 (cf. 2.12–14 and 2.28–30 with 10.8–12 and 10.26).

Venus Where She Belongs: The Arena at Corinth

Readers of Paul's First Letter to the Corinthians will recall that the city was noted for its luxurious tastes and wanton habits. It is an especially appropriate setting for the pantomime of the Judgment of Paris.[70] The implications of the representation of this myth are so obvious, and Apuleius' own words about the ugly realities underlying the scene are so explicit, that little need be added to what every reader can find in the closing pages of Book 10.[71] The story of Paris causes Lucius, a "philosophizing ass" (10.33), to reflect on other famous errors in human judgment: first Palamedes, Ajax, and the arms of Achilles; then Socrates' trial at Athens. By this association, Apuleius points his readers toward the moral of the scene. The Judgment of Paris

---

69. For a history of this type in Latin literature, see Georg Luck, *Hexen und Zauberei in der römischen Dichtung* (Zurich, 1962).

70. See H. J. Mason, "Lucius at Corinth," *Phoenix* 25 (1971), 160–165.

71. The arena's spectacle provided the Christians with a conveniently gory theme with which to attack paganism; cf. Tertullian, *On the Public Shows* 21: ". : . he who shudders at the body of a person who died by natural causes—that same man will in the amphitheater look down with most tolerant eyes on bodies torn and mangled and defiled with their own blood."

symbolizes the inadequacy of human understanding of Venus and her charms.

Two more points about the arena scene deserve special emphasis. The first is that Paris' judgment and the ensuing triumph of Venus are uncommonly appropriate to climax Lucius' own education in the nature of human desires. Recall the sequel to the Judgment of Paris: never was the temptation to yield to sensual pleasure stronger than that offered by Venus; and never was the outcome of yielding to temptation more calamitous than the event that followed—the Trojan War.

Second, the arena scene strikes a chord quite familiar from earlier episodes in the novel. As in the contrast of Psyche's wedding with the punishment envisioned for Lucius and Charite at the end of Book 6, the insinuating, gorgeous pantomime of Venus and Paris at the end of Book 10 represents a harsh contrast with the scene soon to be enacted in the arena. No wishful thinking should dispel that dissonance. For Lucius the moment is at once humiliating and dangerous.[72] What is most frightening of all is that Venus' powers are now to be turned into an instrument of punishment. Here is an execution through the act of love.

Nothing that has gone before exposes the illusory nature of the beguiling, "earthly" Venus quite so starkly as the arena at Corinth. For Lucius at least this last prospect is too much. He has no choice but to flee for his life. He reaches Cenchreae, "safest of harbors," but it remains to be seen where his flight will lead beyond that.

BOOK 11

Lucius is awakened by the brilliant light of the moon (1). Exhausted by his journeying and in despair of ever being saved from his endless round of misfortunes, he prays to the Queen of Heaven, revealed in the moon, for release from his beastly form

---

72. See 10.35: Lucius' vivid imagination leads him to have less concern for his shame (*pudor*) than for his personal safety (*salus*).

(2). No sooner does he fall back into deep sleep than a miraculous vision of Isis appears in answer to his prayers (3–4). Moved by his suffering and his entreaties, she foretells an end to his imprisonment in the body of an ass and asks him to spend the rest of his life in devoted service to her (5–6). The sun rises and Lucius witnesses a splendid procession of Isis' devotees (8–11). Following the instructions of the goddess, a priest steps forward with a wreath of roses. Lucius eats them and is at once changed back into his human form (14). A priest of Isis then explains to the bystanders the history of Lucius prior to this moment and declares that Lucius' life will henceforth be dedicated to the service of Isis; the more fully he enters into her service, the more abundantly will he reap the fruit of his newly won liberty (15). Lucius is reunited with his family, servants, and friends (18–19). He is then initiated further into Isis' mysteries by the priest Mithras and renders elaborate thanks to her for his salvation (20–25). He goes to Rome, where he worships at Isis' shrine (the temple of Isis Campensis) and is initiated into the religion of the supreme father of all the gods, Osiris (26). Near the end of the story it is revealed that Lucius is in fact from Madauros, Apuleius' native city (27). Fortified by the power of Isis and Osiris, he will rise rapidly to the forefront of the legal profession in Rome and will never need to fear the slanders of those envious of his immense learning and experience (27–28). He enters into a college of *pastophors* and as a decurion proudly wears the robe and tonsure of a priest in the service of Isis (30).

A Great Daimōn Appears

The rise of the moon signals that Isis is about to intervene in Lucius' life.[73] The prayer he addresses to the Queen of Heaven is in the form of an invocation to a deity whose name he does not know, to an *agnostos theos*. But he has absolute confidence that her power will be able to change his life. When Isis does

---

73. Cf. Artemidorus (fl. 2d century after Christ) 2.39: "For these gods (sc. of Egypt) have always been regarded as the saviors of men who have tried every resort and who find themselves in utmost peril... they indicate immediate salvation for those who are already in a difficult situation" (*The Interpretation of Dreams*, trans. Robert J. White [Park Ridge, N.J., 1975]). On Book 11 generally, see the commentaries of Fredouille and Griffiths.

appear, she promises to do exactly that. Her miraculous appearance to Lucius begins the *Navigium Isidis,* or *Ploiaphesia,* a festival that inaugurates the sailing season of the Roman New Year in early March. The time is appropriate for Lucius' rebirth as a servant of Isis, as is the setting at Cenchreae, "safest of harbors for ships"; recent archaeological excavations have revealed an actual shrine to Isis there.

Most of Book 11 is given over to a celebration of Lucius' return to human form and the beginning of a new life in the service of Isis. Relief sculptures from the second and third centuries provide us with some impression of the ceremonial parade described in 11.8–10. Figure 11 shows a stylized representation of the kind of procession Lucius sees on waking from his dream vision. In Figure 12 we see a leading figure, Anubis (identified by the jackal's head), and the festive pipes and cult symbols of the other figures. One detail in Apuleius' description not represented in either illustration is the fake Pegasus, the ass with wings pasted to his sides (11.8). This is yet another playful contrast between the ass and more exalted creatures from mythology (cf. the ironic references to Pegasus and Bellerophon at 6.30, 7.26, and 8.16).

The Providence of Isis

In the middle of Book 11, the priest of Isis delivers a speech interpreting Lucius' career at the hands of Fortune and his deliverance into the care of "seeing Fortune," Isis. Every word uttered by the priest is of the utmost import. He is, in effect, providing the novel's (Apuleius') interpretation of Lucius' experiences. Book 11 has long been a major sourcebook for the history of religions. For readers of *The Golden Ass,* the priest's words are, like the transformation scene in Book 3, so important that they must be quoted in their entirety. Immediately before being transformed back into a man, Lucius finds himself faced with a crown of roses, the magical antidote to Pamphile's ointment:

And by Hercules it was a crown, since by the providence of the greatest of goddesses, after so many exhausting hardships, after so many enor-

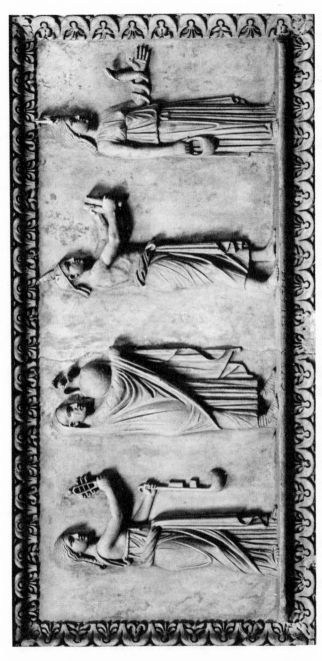

11. Procession of Isis worshipers. Musei Vaticani, Rome. Reproduced by permission of the Deutsches Archäologisches Institut, Rome. Photograph by Anderson.

12. Procession of Isis worshipers led by figure with the head of Anubis. Museum at Klein-Glienecke bei Potsdam. Reproduced by permission of F. W. Goethert, Berlin.

mous dangers, I would conquer Fortune, who had so savagely fought against me. [11.12]

The priest's first words echo these thoughts of Lucius.[74] We have come full circle. As with the tale of Aristomenes, Lucius is once again hearing things he has himself said or had in mind to say.[75] But there is an important difference between this passage and such earlier ones as Aristomenes' tale or Lucius' own pretty fables in books 9 and 10. The priest's sermon on fortune, providence, and curiosity is distinguished by its total lack of irony and deception:

After many exhausting hardships, after the great storms of Fortune, after her greatest tempests, driven though you were, at long last, Lucius, have you reached your port of Repose and your altar of Mercy. Neither your noble birth nor your dignified position nor even learning, in which you excel, have benefited you in any way. No, falling into the slavery of pleasure, in the wantonness of your greening youth, you reaped the unhappy reward for your inauspicious curiosity. Yet even so, blind Fortune, while she tortured you with the worst dangers, has in her improvident malice brought you to this very state of religious beatitude. Let her go now and rage with all her fury, let her find some other object for her cruelty. For those people whose lives the majesty of our goddess has claimed for her own service, for them dire calamity has no place. What gain did wicked Fortune derive from bandits, what from wild beasts, what from slavery, long, hard labor on the road, what from wandering here and there on the hardest of journies, what from the fear of death to which you were daily exposed? Now you have been taken into the protection of Fortune, but of a Fortune who can see, who with the splendor of her light even illuminates the other gods.[76] Put on therefore a more joyful countenance, one that befits that white garment you wear; follow with a renewed step the procession of the goddess who saves you. Let those without religion see, let them see their error

___

74. Cf. the Latin of 11.12 ("... quod ac tantis exanclatis laboribus, tot emensis periculis deae maximae providentia adluctantem mihi saevissime Fortunam superarem") with the opening of 11.15 ("multis et variis exanclatis laboribus...").

75. See the earlier discussion of the witty tale in my remarks on Book 1.

76. "In tutelam iam receptus es Fortunae, sed videntis, quae suae lucis splendore ceteros iam deos illuminat" (11.15). We need only refer back to Lucius' complaints about Fortune at 7.2–3 to appreciate the dramatic impact of *sed videntis*.

and acknowledge it: behold, now, freed from his former miseries by the great providence of Isis, Lucius glories in his Fortune! All the same, so that you may be the safer and better fortified, give your name to this sacred soldiery, whose sacrament you will hereafter never question, and dedicate yourself now to the service of our religion and take up the voluntary yoke of this ministry. For when you have begun to be a slave of the goddess, then will you all the more reap the fruit of your liberty. [11.15]

The priest draws on all the major themes of the novel, and his theology also provides an instructive parallel for the literary qualities of Lucius' tale. The contrast between the *sermo Milesius* of Books 1–10 and Book 11 is enormous, but it is no greater than the contrast between the world of Fortuna caeca, blind Fortune, and the blessed new world of Fortuna videns, Isis.

The last half of Book 11 is devoted to Lucius' account of his initiation into the mysteries of Isis. Her intercession enables him to come to know the highest of all gods, Osiris. Although he is described as the supreme god, his cult was in fact negligible compared to that of Isis. Hence Lucius merely acknowledges Osiris' supremacy (11.27).

Later, in Rome, Lucius is admitted to the temple of Isis Campensis (Isis-in-the-Fields), a site in the Campus Martius familiar to us from earlier Latin works, in which it was associated with sexual license. As far as Apuleius is concerned, the site is now quite respectable. Yet the fervor of Book 11 has no parallel in Roman literature of earlier days. In Rome, it was the women that worshiped Isis, and that fact provided a theme for the Latin elegiac poets (e.g., the lover's complaint about Isis in Tibullus, 1.3.23–32, and the prayer to Isis to heal a mistress who has undergone an abortion in Ovid, *Amores* 2.13). A sterner testimony is Juvenal's sneering reference to the Iseum in the Campus Martius and his mocking account of an Isis procession (6.511–541).[77]

---

77. See Georg Wissowa, *Religion und Kultus der Römer, Handbuch der klassischen Altertumswissenschaft*, pt. 5, vol. 4 (Munich, 1902), 351–358, and Reinhold Merkelbach, *Isisfeste in griechisch-römischer Zeit* (Meisenheim am Glam, 1963). Walsh has suggested that Book 11 might also be designed to counter the rising appeal of Christianity (*Roman Novel*, 187)—presumably through seduction rather than polemic.

13. Isis-Fortuna. Museo Nazionale, Naples. The rudder and cornucopia signify the goddess Fortuna. Reproduced by permission of the Deutsches Archäologisches Institut, Rome.

As Lucius' odyssey to Queen Isis draws to a close, allusions to the envy and slander of the ignorant, irreligious masses seem to suggest that Apuleius himself may be peeking through the fabric of his novel; certainly the allusion by the priest in Rome to the "poor Madauran" encourages us to believe that something like Lucius' conversion happened to Apuleius (11.27, 11.30). The unexpected reference to Madauros is an identifying "seal" (termed in Greek poetry a *sphragis*) that dramatically reveals a book's author. The indirection in Book 11 is typical of Apuleius' narrative technique. As we shall see in following chapters, the author of the *Apology* and *Florida* would not have objected to being identified with the noble young man—so distinguished by his learning, so comely in appearance—whose spiritual purity earns the intervention of Isis and the salvation that intervention ensures.

The Moral of The Golden Ass

Is it desirable to attempt to ascribe a moral to a work as long and complex as *The Golden Ass?* I think so. The priest of Isis is willing to do as much for Lucius' experiences at 11.15; and, provided we do not mistake a relatively simple summation for a comment on the literary complexity of Apuleius' tale, the effort at least may clarify our understanding of Book 11—in many ways so radical a departure from the tone and spirit of the rest of Lucius' story.

The conversion of Lucius, like his retransformation to his human form, is due to Isis and to no one else. Like Psyche, he has required the intervention of a high being, a *mesitēs* or *daimōn*, to save him from his natural state. The very man who wished to know "everything or as much as possible" now enjoins us, his readers, from indulging our curiosity (11.23). Yet has he really learned from his experiences? As with Psyche, we are not permitted to know the answer to the question. Whether Lucius has learned his lesson or no, he at least is prepared to give a lesson to us: the curiosity about which he speaks is an appetite to know everything and leave nothing unexplained. As Philo Judaeus pointed out long before Apuleius was born, to indulge that kind of curiosity will lead only to aimless conjecture and a great deal more harm than good:

> For the great darkness that covers the world of bodies and of affairs does not allow us to see the nature of each thing; and though someone overpowered by curiosity or love of learning might wish to peer through that darkness, it is exactly like a blind man who stumbles over obstacles before he grasps them, then loses his footing and misses his aim; or, if his hands do lay hold of something, he infers from uncertainties and has not truth but conjecture in his grasp. [*On Drunkenness* 167]

It is precisely this kind of blindness that brings about the labors and sufferings of Lucius. Philo characterizes such labors succinctly: "The toil that springs from unintelligence is miserable and full of affliction, just as that which has intelligence for its parent is profitable" (*On the Changing of Names* 193). When we compare Lucius with an Aeneas, or even with the hero to whom he likens himself, Odysseus, we can see a crucial difference. Lucius' travails are endless and in a sense meaningless, because they accomplish nothing and lead nowhere. Odysseus' aim was to set his house and kingdom once again in order; and Aeneas' mission was to found Rome. The most Lucius can aim to do is save himself, and thanks to Isis, he finally succeeds in that mission. Few persons in his day would hope for more.

Now Lucius rejoices in his life as a *pastophor* of Isis. He is joined with god, and, like Psyche at the end of her story, he is filled with joy at his deliverance.[78] Figure 14 shows a bronze statuette of a priest of Isis in the Louvre. Apuleius' description of Lucius might have inspired its artist, so closely does this statuette reflect the asceticism and devotion that abound at the end of *The Golden Ass*. The little priest's simplicity is worlds away from the sensuous *voluptates* of Lucius' earlier life—in particular such pleasure as he once took in the beauties of the flesh. Recall the encomium on hair inspired by Fotis (2.8). As is shown

78. Cf. the final words of the novel, *gaudens obibam* (11.30), "rejoicing I went forth," with the close of Psyche's tale: Psyche's daughter is named Voluptas, Joy or Pleasure, and is born of the union of Soul with divine Love. The full meaning of the old woman's tale is realized only in the final pages of the novel.

14. An Egyptian priest. Bronze statuette. Reproduced by permission of the Musée du Louvre, Paris. Photograph by Maurice Chuzeville.

in his sensuous description of Isis' hair (11.3–4), Lucius even now does not scorn that kind of beauty. His shaved head is only the symbol of a voluntary servitude enjoined on every believer in Isis.[79]

Lucius' entry into the service of Isis may be compared with the lot that Socrates says befell Odysseus:

> It chanced that the soul of Odysseus drew the last lot of all and came forward to make its choice; with the memory of its former toils it flung away ambition and wandered for a long time in search of the life of a private citizen who stayed out of others' business. And with difficulty it found that life lying somewhere, neglected by the others. And when it saw it, it said it would have done the same even if it had drawn the first lot. And it chose that life gladly. [Plato, *Republic* 10.620C–D]

Only an Odysseus—that is, only a man of sufficient experience and understanding of the world—is capable of choosing a life such as Lucius elects in Book 11. That new life will be marked by a spiritual simplicity—combined, let us not forget, with a successful career as a lawyer. May not that part of Apuleius which was the Platonic philosopher have had the same hope for his Grecian tale that Socrates expressed for the myth of Er?

> And so, Glaucon, the tale was saved and did not die, and it would save us, would we be persuaded by it; and we shall easily cross the river of Lethe and not stain our soul with this world. But if we are persuaded by me, believing that the soul is immortal and has the power to withstand all kinds of evil and all kinds of good, we shall hold always to the upward way and pursue justice with wisdom in every way, so that we may be dear to ourselves and to the gods, both during our time here and when we receive our rewards in the manner of the prizewinners in the games who go about gathering their prizes. Thus, both here and in that journey of a thousand years that I have explained to you, we shall fare well. [Plato, *Republic* 10.621B–D]

79. See 11.15, "nam cum coeperis deae servire, tunc magis senties fructum tuae libertatis" ("for when you have begun to be a slave to the goddess, then will you all the more reap the fruit of your liberty").

CHAPTER 3

The Notoriety of
the Milesian Tale

The good ended happily and the bad unhappily. That is what
Fiction means.

—Oscar Wilde, *The Importance of*
Being Earnest, Act 2

1

Such was Lucius' odyssey toward Queen Isis. His story has
obvious affinities with other novels that survive from antiquity,
above all in the way he is buffeted about by Fortune in the first
ten books. But there are also some important differences. The
plot of a typical Greek romance tends to develop along the following lines:

The protagonists are a young man and woman invariably described as the most beautiful—if not always the wisest—of
mortals. In all other respects they are like everyone else, as far
removed from the heroic stature of a Jason or a Medea as ordinary people could be. Because of their good looks, they excite
the jealousy of other people, and quite often of a god. Soon after
their story begins they are separated, sometimes immediately
after celebrating their marriage. A poignant touch often contrived is that they are parted before the marriage is consum-
mated. The bride is usually abducted by pirates or bandits, and
eventually so is the bridegroom. They undergo all kinds of
adventures—usually separately, sometimes together—but they
rarely suffer more than temporarily spoiled good looks: a shaven
head, dirty clothes, or the stripes from a beating. Both hero and
heroine must fend off a variety of approaches from those who
are bewitched by their beauty. Usually each must contend with

proposals from both sexes. Yet despite many temptations, the sanctity of conjugal love is maintained. It is particularly important that the young woman preserve her chastity. Frustrated suitors are sometimes driven to throw their lives away in despair. The heroine suffers one or more "false deaths," in which she appears to have been slain but miraculously survives to face further perils. The more improbable the dangers, the better. There are fires, shipwrecks, kidnappings, temporary fits of insanity, servitude, attacks by wild beasts, murders, and any other hurdle the author can think of. Then the pair are reunited. A patron deity usually reveals its role at the end, perhaps a goddess particularly beloved of women, such as Isis or Aphrodite.

The basis for using the word *romance* to refer to this kind of fiction will be quickly apparent.[1] In every Greek novel the licentious *amores* such as those that abound in *The Golden Ass* are only so many afflictions that hero and heroine are eventually well rid of, rather like the measles. But Apuleius is concerned with something far different from the romantic love of the Greek novels we know. The many false trails and disappointments in the stories of Plotina and Charite in Books 7 and 8 impart a bitterly ironic twist to the sentimental conventions of those tales.

Much the same could be said of the relationship of Petronius' *Satyricon* to the conventions of Greek fiction. Even if the *Satyricon* is not a direct parody of the five complete novels that survive, it clearly burlesques the ideals of those latter-day odysseys.[2] To find everything a Greek romance could never be, to see its most typical feature—a faithful heterosexual couple—turned inside out as a faithless mob of homosexual lovers, one

1. The Greeks for once lacked a word for something—or at least they did not use ours; the word *novel*, for example, derives from the *novelle*, or short stories, of Boccaccio's *Decameron*. The ancients were content with such general terms as *plasma* (fiction) and *genomena* (things that happen, events). See B. P. Reardon, "The Greek Novel," *Phoenix* 23 (1969), 291–309, and "Aspects of the Greek Novel," *Greece and Rome* 23 (1976), 118–131.

2. Typical motifs in the early literature are examined in Sophie Trenkner, *The Greek Novella in the Classical Period* (Cambridge, 1958).

need follow the "romance" of Giton, Encolpius, and Ascyltus only briefly.[3]

Petronius' works also differs markedly from those of Apuleius, but in another way. However alike their odyssean narratives may seem in pace and structure, there is a profound difference of spirit. That difference can be seen by referring to a passage from each that is of considerable thematic importance. Let us turn first to an elegiac poem from *Satyricon* 132 which reduces Epicurus' doctrine on pleasure to little more than vulgar hedonism. The ideas are a fair summary of the outlook on life of the narrator, Encolpius:

> quid me constricta spectatis fronte Catones
>   damnatisque novae simplicitatis opus?
> sermonis puri non tristis gratia ridet,
>   quodque facit populus, candida lingua refert.
> nam quis concubitus, Veneris quis gaudia nescit?
>   quis vetat in tepido membra calere toro?
> ipse pater veri doctos Epicurus amare
>   iussit et hoc vitam dixit habere *telos*.

Why do you watch me with furrowed brow, you Catos, and condemn my work of modern simplicity? A grace of pure speech, not sad, smiles, and relates whatever people do with a frank tongue. For who does not know sex, who does not know the joys of Venus? Who disdains to warm his limbs on a cozy couch? The father of truth himself, Epicurus, commanded his disciples to love, and said that life had this as its goal.

Epicurus said nothing of the kind. There is a splendid diatribe against this view of sex in Lucretius, 4.1058–1287. Nor is it wise to assume that these lines actually reflect Petronius' own views.

---

3. This comment is not intended to revive the old theory that Petronius actually satirized any one of the five complete Greek romances that have been handed down to us. All of them were written after his death in A.D. 65. But sweetness, sentimentality, and naiveté are typical qualities of the protagonists of a Greek romance, and none of these traits are to be found in the *urbanitas* or sophistication of the *Satyricon*. See Albert Henrichs, *Die Phoinikika des Lollianus: Fragmente eines neuen Griechischen Romans*, Papyrologische Texte and Abhandlungen 14 (Bonn, 1972), 19–23.

Usually when his characters preach in this fashion we can be sure we need not take what they say at face value; see the exchange between Encolpius and the windbag rhetorician Agamemnon on the corruption of education (1–5) and the remarks of the poet Eumolpus on the poverty of his art (83–84), followed by good evidence of the reasons for its decline (118–124).

However one cares to interpret *Satyricon* 132, Apuleius looks at the world with a very different eye. No better passage could be adduced to illustrate this point than these words of Isis to Lucius:

Only remember and keep the memory fast in your heart that all the remaining course of your life is dedicated to me, up to the very moment that you draw your last breath. Nor is it at all amiss that you should owe everything in your life to her by whose kindness you will return to the world of men. Rather you shall live blessed, you shall live glorious within my protection; and when you have measured out the span of your life and gone down to the dead, even in that hidden sphere of the earth you shall see me shining amidst the shadows of Acheron and reigning in the Stygian depths; there you shall dwell in the Elysian fields, continually adoring me for my favor. Then if by your sedulous devotion, dutiful ceremony, and constant chastity you prove deserving of my divinity, you will learn that it is even within my power to extend your span of life beyond the limits that have been set for it by fate. [11.6]

The contrast should be clear: on the one hand a casual hedonism, a mere perversion of Epicurus' far from simple teachings on the nature of pleasure;[4] on the other, an expression of faith in the very kind of religion the Epicureans traditionally regarded as a comforting illusion (see Lucretius, 1.62–101, 5.1194–1240). Even in their ways of writing Latin the two authors are worlds apart. Petronius' frank speech and modern simplicity embody a style quite alien to the precious, archaized Latin of the second century. Apuleius, even though he might have reported candidly the thoughts expressed by his contem-

4. See J. M. Rist, *Epicurus: An Introduction* (Cambridge, 1972), 100–126.

poraries, wrote a kind of Latin that drew heavily on the texts of such suitably archaic authors as Plautus.[5]

Yet despite their divergent styles and differing views of the world, the names of Petronius and Apuleius came to be linked in an important way, and justly so. Petronius' reputation was not greatly harmed by the fact that he wrote a "Milesian narrative." For Apuleius the consequences of doing so were different.

2

Greek novelists might pose as erotic historians or letter writers.[6] Since the beginning and end of the *Satyricon* are lost, it is impossible to be sure what Petronius thought of his work beyond that suspect "message" in *Satyricon* 132. But in his opening sentence Apuleius speaks of weaving his varied stories together into a "Milesian narrative" (*sermone isto Milesio*), and that is a surprising turn of phrase. As nearly as we can determine, Milesian tales were famous in antiquity for all the wrong reasons.

Aristides of Miletus invented the genre in the second century B.C., and the Roman Cornelius Sisenna translated some tales into Latin a century later. With only these meager facts to go on, the early history of the Milesian tale cannot be easily written; very little survives from Aristides and Sisenna except a scandalous reputation and a few fragments; for example, the single Greek word *Milesiaka*, Milesian stories.[7] In what follows we shall be dealing mainly with the invidious reputation of the Milesian tale—the reviews rather than the works themselves.

Petronius and Apuleius furnish our only samples of this Greek invention. A brief anecdote in Plutarch's *Life of Crassus* can tell us something about their character. This important testimony comes via the Parthians, of all people. At the Battle of Carrhae in 55 B.C. they killed 20,000 Romans and captured some 10,000 more. One of their generals, Surena, cut off the head and

---

5. The language of *The Golden Ass* is discussed in greater detail in Chapter 5.

6. For an epistolary philosophical novel, see Ingemar Düring, *Chion of Heraclea* (Gothenburg, 1951).

7. All the evidence for the development of this literary genre is reviewed in P. G. Walsh, *The Roman Novel: The Satyricon of Petronius and the Metamorphoses of Apuleius* (Cambridge, 1970), 10–18.

right hand of the triumvir Crassus; afterward, while plundering
the baggage of the Romans, he made an interesting discovery:

> Before the assembled senate of Seleucia, Surena carried in the scandal-
> ous books of the *Milesian Stories* of Aristides. In this instance at least he
> was telling the truth, because the books had been found in the baggage
> of Roscius. They gave Surena an occasion to heap much insulting
> ridicule on the Romans for not being able to let such subjects and
> literature alone even when they went to war. [Plutarch, *Life of Cras-
> sus 32*]

While no one would take Surena for an ideal literary critic, what
could Aristides' *Milesian Stories* have been like to cause him to
forget even the worries of a day like Carrhae? The Parthians
were not the last readers of Milesian tales to be scandalized. It
might also be said in defense of their literary acumen that they
could have been more than a little hypocritical on this occasion.
Plutarch, drawing a connection between the literary genre and
the city of its origins, continues by observing: "Roscius was of
course at fault, but it was shameless for the Parthians to condemn these *Milesian Stories* when many of the royal Arsarcids
were descendants of courtesans from Miletus and Ionia" (32).
Since hypocrisy and genuine moral outrage are easily mistaken
for one another, it is a relief not to have to decide which was
operative in this instance. More remarkable than the Parthians'
possible duplicity is the way they managed to achieve such extremes of savagery and prudery within the space of a single day.
     Plutarch's story about Roscius' bedtime reading is not con-
tradicted by Petronius or Apuleius. Their tales also treat of sexual adventures, with an occasional account of the supernatural,
and they are never less than indelicate. The lewdness of these
stories is often remarked upon. Deserving of equal emphasis is
the limited range of themes, at least in the work of Petronius and
Apuleius: a tale usually appeals either to the sensual appetites
or, less often, to superstition. This is not a pretentious art form.
     Now for Petronius to write such fare was not particularly dis-
turbing. Unlike Apuleius, he was no self-styled Platonic
philosopher. He had no grandiose reputation to compromise.
Quite the opposite is suggested by Tacitus' famous characteriza-

tion of him in the *Annals*. Petronius' virtuosity as a scientist of pleasures never interfered with his duties as consul and proconsul:

He was a man who passed his days sleeping and his nights working or enjoying life. Just as hard work exalts some, so did idleness win him a reputation. He was not regarded as a prodigal voluptuary, as are most of those who squander their money, but as a man of refined luxury. The more abandoned he was in word and deed, and the more these things argued a certain negligence about him, so much the more was it all taken as the charming appearance of the unstudied personality. [*Annals* 16.18]

In the *Satyricon* Milesian tales are recounted by such humble characters as the freedmen Niceros and Trimalchio and the wandering bard Eumolpus, whose stories about the boy of Pergamum and the widow of Ephesus express perfectly the character of their narrator (*Satyricon* 85–87, 110.6–113.2). For Eumolpus handsome boys and beautiful women succumb to lust inevitably: *così fan tutte*. Much the same interpretation of human foibles is evident in Apuleius' tales.

As a literary form, then, Milesian tales are no more pretentious than a Greek pantomime or a comedy of Plautus; in view of their typical morals, they are usually a good deal less respectable than either. They goad readers on to ever higher levels of urbanity by an almost monotonously low estimation of human character. When compared to the idealized romances of Greek fiction, they exhibit a similar kind of idealization—if in the opposite direction. The Milesian tales of Petronius and Apuleius are as ideally cynical in their way as a Greek romance such as *Daphnis and Chloe* is idealistic and sentimental.

As we turn to those remarks from antiquity that link Apuleius' name directly with his Milesian tales, we must not attempt to gloss over the significance of what he says in the opening chapter of *The Golden Ass*. These later references are never favorable. Like the anecdote in Plutarch, they suggest that reading or writing Milesian tales was the mark of a depraved character— suitable material, in fact, for political invective. The historian Julius Capitolinus writes in the *Historia Augusta* of the would-be emperor Clodius Albinus (killed in 197) that he was gluttonous and licentious and wrote Milesian tales "of average quality." Julius reproduces a letter of the emperor Septimius Severus complaining to the Senate about its preferment of Clodius Albinus. Toward the end of the letter Severus scornfully refers to Albinus' patrimony and concludes with some remarks on the unfortunate literary tastes of his enemy:

It was an even greater sorrow for me that many of you regard him as deserving of praise for his literary taste, when actually he spent his time in worthless pastimes, dissipating himself in the Milesian stories from Carthage written by his author Apuleius, and in other literary trifles. [Life of Clodius Albinus 12]

We may reasonably assume that this last thrust was not meant to be a light one. While the historicity of this letter is doubtful, the criticism does reflect the opinion evidently prevailing in antiquity toward Milesian tales as an "unserious" enterprise.[8] The possibility that Lucius' story could be a barely disguised account of Apuleius' own experiences does nothing to alter the implications of this unfavorable notice from the Historia Augusta.

St. Augustine appears to have known Apuleius' writings quite well; in the main he used them as a ready source of Platonic doctrine. In a discussion of metempsychosis and other magical transformations, Augustine remarks:

Men's minds are not turned into those of beasts, but rather a human intelligence is retained, just as Apuleius said happened to him in the work he entitled The Golden Ass. There he says that by the use of a drug he was turned into an ass, but retained his human mind. He either reported this as it actually happened or made it up. [The City of God 18.18]

Augustine is not concerned with the propriety of Apuleius' novel and doubts that a Christian should put any faith in such stories: "These things are either so untrue or so unusual that

8. See R. Syme, Emperors and Biography: Studies in the Historia Augusta (Oxford, 1971), 62–63, for the literary activities that Julius Capitolinus ascribes to Albinus.

they might well not be believed in" (18.18). He is in the midst of a lengthy refutation of the existence of Platonic *daimones*, those intermediate beings that exist between gods and human beings; for this purpose Apuleius' treatise *On the God of Socrates* furnished a convenient source. The above passage is incidentally the earliest known use of the alternate title *The Golden Ass*.

Finally, the fourth-century Platonist Macrobius provides us with our most direct criticism of Apuleius' writing of Milesian tales. In his commentary on Cicero's *Dream of Scipio*, he prefaces his main text with a discussion of the various types of myths, in an effort to distinguish those appropriate for philosophy. Macrobius follows a commentary on the *Republic*'s myth of Er by the Greek Proclus and repeats a criticism of Plato made by the Epicurean Colotes:

Colotes says that no philosopher is justified in making up a story, since no kind of fiction befits those who profess the truth. "For why," he says, "if you wish to teach us an idea of heavenly things and the place of men's souls, why is that not done with a simple and pure approach, but instead with an assumed character and a novelty of events all thought up, with a scene composed of imaginary characters, all of which pollute with a lie the very door to truth which you are seeking?" [*Commentary* 1.2]

Colotes would be every bit as critical of Cicero as he was of Plato. As Macrobius remarks, Colotes' carping would disturb even the dream of Scipio Africanus.

Colotes' strictures can be refuted by some useful distinctions in regard to the didactic value of myth—distinctions of which Apuleius, of course, was well aware.[9] Not every kind of myth is appropriate to philosophy, but some deserve to be used and by no means deserve Colotes' scorn:

The very word "tales" shows that they are professions of an untruth.[10] They are invented either only for the pleasure of lulling one's audience

9. See *On the God of Socrates* (Prologue, 4), where Apuleius makes a point by telling Aesop's fable of the crow and the fox.

10. The etymology connects *fabula* ("tale," "fictitious story") and *fabulari* ("to invent a story," "make up a fable").

or for the sake of urging them on to good works as well. They beguile the listener in the same way as comedies, of the sort that Menander and his imitators produced for performance, or, again, as the plots told about the imaginary vicissitudes of lovers, in which kind of work Petronius so indulged himself, and in which Apuleius also sometimes dallied—to our astonishment. [*Commentary* 1.2]

Aesop's fables could harm no one. A philosopher would be quite justified in referring to them or to some other improving stories to convey doctrines that are difficult or unwelcome at first hearing. Macrobius' reply to Colotes is especially sensible when we remember that no less an Epicurean than Lucretius used the honeyed language of poetry as a means of teaching his master's doctrine (Lucretius, 2.398–401).

With the possible exception of the allegory of Cupid and Psyche, however, Apuleius' Milesian tales would never be mistaken for either Platonic myth or Aesopian fable. Macrobius would seem to have placed Apuleius quite accurately where he belongs, as far as the character of his *fabulae* is concerned. Nor is that all. Macrobius characterized *fabulae* in the same way that Apuleius did, and even used terminology similar to Apuleius' words in the opening sentence of *The Golden Ass*, where he promised to delight and astound the reader: "Auresque tuas benevolas... permulceam" (Apuleius); "Fabulae... conciliandae auribus voluptatis gratia repertae sunt... auditum mulcent" (Macrobius). Apuleius kept that promise, and in Macrobius' view he compromised his reputation by doing so.[11]

3

From even this brief survey of the evidence, it is difficult to avoid the conclusion that Apuleius described his novel in such a way as virtually to guarantee its being taken for a piece of triviality; for trivial the Milesian tale would surely seem when compared to such respectable works as orations or philosophical treatises. But as we saw in Chapter 2, *The Golden Ass* also expresses in Book 11 an evidently sincere and powerful evange-

---

11. B. E. Perry, *The Ancient Romances: A Literary-Historical Account of Their Origins*, Sather Classical Lectures 37 (Berkeley, 1967), 244.

lism; the "entertainment" of the Milesian narrative tends with ever clearer irony toward a philosophy of life that turns away from the enticements that abound in the first ten books; and there is reasonably good evidence that Apuleius took pains to arrange the entire novel in a coherent way, so that it would be possible for him simultaneously to entertain and to edify his audience by his complex story. Do all these seemingly contradictory elements really combine into a single, coherent whole?

More than one reader has argued that they do not. The most representative critic of this kind is B. E. Perry. For him, the circumstances of the novel's composition are a decisive factor:

> With his showman's instinct for the value of immediate dramatic effects (which often leads him into self-contradiction elsewhere), he feels that all he needs to do in order to prevent the publication of his old wives' tales from becoming a scandal in the literary world, comparable to that of Aristides' *Milesiaca*, is to make a personal appearance on the stage in the last act, bow deeply and reverently before his audience, and overwhelm them with the magic of his eloquence on a subject of grave and universal import, a subject about which he speaks with earnest conviction and sincerity, but which does not belong with the story of Lucius. Deeply impressed with the solemnity of this final act, his public will go away without thinking about the nature of what went before, and thereby two objects will have been achieved: the author will have delivered, in the form of "Milesian" tales in the first ten chapters, the kind of entertainment with which he knew that his readers would be charmed, in spite of its disrespectability as literature; and, at the same time, his book as a whole will have been redeemed in some measure from the appearance of complete frivolity and from the scorn of his learned contemporaries.[12]

Perry identifies a basic issue cogently enough: what business did St. Augustine's noble Platonist have writing Milesian tales? If Perry's criticism is not much different from the one advanced by Macrobius some 1,500 years before, that is not to say it ought not to be taken seriously.

Part of the answer is that the entertainment in *The Golden Ass* is not always so frivolous or inconsequential as Perry makes out

12. Ibid., 245.

to be. The humor grows progressively darker and more sardonic. Additionally, Apuleius exploits the didactic power inherent in any fictional narrative; a storyteller is no less effective when he relates how bad or misguided persons come to an unhappy end than when he tells of virtue and goodness rewarded. If the novel begins as a Milesian entertainment, it ends with a world utterly transformed and remote from the earlier stories of lust, revenge, or adultery. Aside from a few cryptic signals here and there, Apuleius gives us no hint that anything of the kind is in the offing, and that is not a sign that he is confused or undisciplined, only that he is a good entertainer and a subtle one. He encourages his readers to begin with one understanding of the work, then allows them to discover another purpose beyond simple entertainment beneath the surface of his Milesian story. Apuleius' contemporary Aulus Gellius recommended something like this strategy when he advised that a salutary tale not be told "in the austere and dictatorial manner of philosophers," but rather as an entertaining and witty fable that commends wholesome ideas to its listeners by enticing them effortlessly to hear the truth (*Attic Nights* 2.29). This precept can be seen at work in Apuleius' recital of a fable by Aesop in the prologue to *On the God of Socrates* (4). A little more effort will be required to see why Apuleius might have thought that a Milesian tale would not compromise his reputation as a philosopher.

"Seriousness" and "frivolity" are the time-honored antipodes of Apuleian criticism, yet they are largely subjective terms whose meaning varies from one reader to the next. They also impose far too simplistic alternatives on a work as interesting and complex as *The Golden Ass*. Walsh has described "a central ambivalence in the romance, a tension between Milesian ribaldry and Platonic mysticism, which reflects the complexity of its author's personality."[13] "Ambivalence," at least as a synthesis of "seriousness" and "frivolity," has the merit of avoiding the seesaw of those two terms; yet the artistic personality of Apuleius was not really at war with itself, as will soon be appar-

---

13. Walsh, *Roman Novel*, 143; see also Jean Beaujeu, "Sérieux et frivolité au IIe siècle de notre ère: Apulée," *Bulletin de l'association Guillaume Budé* 4 (1975), 83–97.

ent when we take up some other works written by the man that
B. E. Perry called "Apuleius the showman." "Showman" may
not be an overly complimentary term, but it is much closer to the
truth of the matter than the appellation Apuleius himself would
have preferred us to use—*philosophus Platonicus Madaurensis,*
"Platonic philosopher from Madauros."

CHAPTER 4

An African Socrates

But Aemilianus, more a rustic than the shepherds and
herdsmen in Vergil, ever a bumpkin and barbarian, far more
austere (as he thinks) than your Serranii, Curii, Fabricii, denies
that the kind of verse I have written is worthy of a Platonic
philosopher. Would you say the same, Aemilianus, if I were to
inform you that these lines were composed after the example
of Plato himself?

—Apuleius, *Apology* 10

1

Here we find Apuleius in another role, trying to intimidate
one of his prosecutors with his learning. Nowadays no one
would turn to him for philosophy, unless as the unwitting
transmittor of a genuine philosopher's ideas.[1] Augustine read
Apuleius chiefly because he found his literary digests more ac-
cessible than Plato's Greek.[2] Still, if events were to reveal
Apuleius to be neither as learned as Plutarch nor as original as
Plotinus, he nonetheless convinced many people in antiquity
that he was primarily a philosopher.

No more dramatic evidence for his identification as a
philosopher could be found than the tribute paid him by the
citizens of his native town, Madauros. The archaeological site of
this ancient city lies in eastern Algeria, near the Tunisian bor-
der.[3] In Apuleius' day (ca. 120–190) and down to the lifetime of
Augustine (384–430), Madauros was a thriving center of educa-

1. John Dillon, *The Middle Platonists* (Ithaca, N.Y., 1977), 311.
2. Augustine makes extensive reference to Apuleius; see *On the City of God*
4.2, 8.10–27, 9.2–8.
3. Stéphane Gsell, *Recherches archéologiques en Algérie* (Paris, 1893), 355–358.

15. Portrait of Apuleius on a contorniate medallion struck at Rome in the latter half of the fourth century. See András Alföldi, *Die Kontorniaten* (Budapest and Leipzig, 1943), 137. Bibliothèque Nationale, Paris.

tion and culture; according to Augustine, it was still mostly pagan even in his day (*Letters*, 232.2). During excavations by French archaeologists, a base to a commemorative statue was discovered bearing a dedication to a "Platonic philosopher."[4] That philosopher is generally assumed to be Apuleius. Restored in part, the inscription reads

4. Stéphane Gsell, *Inscriptions latines de l'Algérie* (Paris, 1922), 1.2115.

16. Madauros, Apuleius' birthplace. Reproduced by permission of the Deutsches Archäologisches Institut, Rome.

PHILOSOPHO PLATONICO
MADAVRENSES
CIVES
ORNAMENTO
SVO D · D

TO THE PLATONIC PHILOSOPHER
THE JEWEL IN THEIR CROWN
THE CITIZENS OF MADAUROS
DEDICATE THIS STATUE

A few letters appearing in a second stone fragment may indicate that Apuleius held religious office; for example, "... RPETV ..." might be restored to "[FLAMEN PE] RPETV[VS]." Madauros was not the only city to honor him in this way. We have Apuleius' speech of thanks to the citizens and senate of Carthage for another statue that was to be erected in his honor (*Florida* 16).[5] In the age of the sophists it was not unusual for a famous man to be commemorated by a statue; Philostratus reports a similar honor for Lollianus, a contemporary of Apuleius (*Lives of the Sophists*, 527). In the case of Apuleius, however, we have to do with a rather special case. What did he mean by calling himself a "Platonic philosopher" when, as it happens, he was nothing of the kind? And what exactly was it that his fellow townsmen were celebrating? It was not, as we shall presently discover, his logic or his metaphysics.

The *Apology*, the best known of Apuleius' works after *The Golden Ass*, is a reply to charges of misconduct in his marriage to an older woman. His opponents appear to have attempted to make the study of philosophy into a liability in the court of law. Since we have only Apuleius' version of the story, there is no way to be sure that his enemies were as inept as he makes them seem. Doubtless he chose whatever would best aid his case and suppressed everything else. As the speech stands, his accusers emerge as among the most stupid litigants to appear in classical oratory—and that distinction is not easily won. Rarely have so

5. See the translation in Appendix 1; cf. also 3.11.

many serious charges been mixed with so much nonsense. The speech becomes an *apologia pro vita sua* rather than an *apologia de magia*. Its author takes pride in being an orator, an African, and a Platonic philosopher.

It had not always been so easy to glory in the last of these attainments. When Tacitus was reckoning up the virtues of his father-in-law, Agricola (died A.D. 93), not the least he found to commend was the sensible way the Romans had of dealing with this typically Greek vice:

I remember that he used to tell us how in his early youth he would have imbibed a keener love of philosophy, beyond what was allowed a

17. North Africa in the second century.

Roman and a senator, if his mother's good sense had not checked his excited and ardent spirit. Of course this was a lofty and aspiring soul that sought with more eagerness than caution the beauty and splendor of great and glorious renown. Soon reason and age tempered him, and he retained from his learning that most difficult of lessons: moderation. [*Agricola* 4]

The Romans had long considered that philosophy was best suited to the carefree days of youth. No mature man of affairs could afford the pastime.[6] Even Cicero, who studied and wrote philosophy assiduously, said as much (*On Moral Duties*, 2.2). Yet he himself alternated between a life of public service and quiet contemplation (often enforced by necessity) so successfully that neither the academy nor the political world ever claimed him entirely as their own. Apuleius likewise enjoyed a diverse career and was honored by such a public office as *sacerdos provinciae*, or priest of the imperial cult, a yearly office established in A.D. 71 (Augustine, *Letters*, 138.19). The world of the Antonine emperors offered few political events as exciting as those of Cicero's day—and therefore fewer opportunities for memorable orations—but it was still possible for a good orator to employ his talents fruitfully. Even an ordinary citizen who could lecture on philosophy's mysteries or other edifying subjects—and do it entertainingly—could expect substantial rewards. The ancient biographer of the sophists, Philostratus, records the lives of dozens of Greeks who prospered in this way. And it is in that very role, as a sophist in the Latin-speaking world, that Apuleius appears to us in his *Apology*.

2

Apuleius was tried before the proconsul Claudius Maximus at Sabratha, some miles to the west of Oea, in A.D. 158–159.[7] From the date of Claudius' tenure in office and from Apuleius' own remark that the proconsul Aemilianus Strabo was his contempo-

6. When Carneades, head of the academy at Athens, visited Rome in 155 B.C., Marcus Cato attacked him as a Greek and a philosopher; Plutarch says that no personal animosity was involved (*Cato*, 22–23).

7. Ronald Syme, "Proconsuls d'Afrique sous Antonin le Pieux," *Revue des études anciennes* 61 (1959), 316 and 318.

18. Sabratha, scene of Apuleius' trial in A.D. 158–159. Reproduced by permission of the Deutsches Archäologisches Institut, Rome.

rary derive most of our conjectures about the chronology of Apuleius' life: that he was born about 120, that his wife was perhaps forty years of age at the time of the trial, and that he may have lived until 190 or even later. A chronology of his surviving works is not easy to establish. We do not know whether the *Apology* was delivered before or after he wrote *The Golden Ass*, for no mention is made of Lucius' story anywhere in Apuleius' other writings. The text of the novel permits only guarded inferences about how much of himself Apuleius put into Lucius' story. A recurrent motif of unjust accusations runs through *The Golden Ass*, and there is also the allusion to the "poor Madauran" toward the end of Book 11. Apuleius may have been enjoying a private joke with those of his readers who knew enough about his career to appreciate such subtleties. Since he nearly always placed himself at center stage in his other works, it would be entirely typical of him to have done the same in the novel. We should not forget that Augustine thought *The Golden Ass* was an autobiography—whether fact or fiction.

The personalities and issues of the trial itself are complicated—a sure sign that a good lawyer has been at work. Figure 19 provides a quick guide to the terrain. Very briefly, the details of the case are these. Apuleius had married a widow named Pudentilla, who was some years older than he. Her son Pontianus, whom Apuleius had known during his student days in Athens, persuaded Apuleius to agree to the marriage as a favor and as a precaution against greedy in-laws, particularly Pontianus' uncle Sicinius Aemilianus and his father-in-law, Herennius Rufinus. Pontianus' younger brother, Pudens, was not yet of age, and the cultivated Apuleius would provide an ideal stepfather for the boy. Unfortunately, old loyalties were forgotten, and if Apuleius was ever regarded as anybody's benefactor, that feeling was soon replaced by charges that he had practiced black magic, that he was a fop and a degenerate, and that he had married Pudentilla for her money. The situation was not improved by Pontianus' sudden death; he appears to have been won over to the side of his uncle Aemilianus shortly beforehand. Although the charge of murder does not seem to have been pressed very far, Pontianus' death did indeed remove an

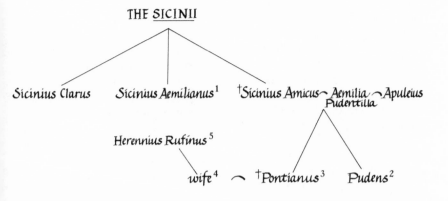

THE SICINII

Sicinius Clarus — Sicinius Aemilianus[1] — †Sicinius Amicus ⌢ Aemilia ⌢ Apuleius Pudentilla

Herennius Rufinus[5]

wife[4] ⌢ †Pontianus[3]   Pudens[2]

⌢ marriage
† death

1 Uncle and guardian of Pudens; co-prosecutor of Apuleius.

2 A young boy at the time of the trial.

3 Apuleius' friend from student days in Athens; urged the marriage to his mother, Pudentilla.

4 Unnamed in the Apology.

5 Pontianus' father-in-law; co-prosecutor of Apuleius.

heir to the family fortune that came with Pudentilla. This turn of events was remarkably advantageous for Apuleius; perhaps his accusers had some justification for bringing their suspicions into court.

We are unlikely ever to know the true outcome of the case, yet the tone of Apuleius' speech is everywhere so assured that it is hard to imagine that he did not win it. It is entirely likely that the action was brought against him because of the money at stake and that the various accusations of magic, philosophy, and depraved living were simply efforts by the prosecution to discredit his character. This procedure was standard in civil trials—it still is. Whatever the merits of the prosecution's charges, Apuleius' speech reads as if civilization itself were on trial. The vital issues became totally lost in a thicket of erudition. The *Apology* is the speech of a man who took the charges of his prosecutors no more seriously than he did their intelligence, which he scorned as nonexistent. The words he attributed to them seem to support that opinion:

"We accuse you of being a handsome philosopher, one who is extremely accomplished in Greek as well as Latin!" Would that such heavy charges against my appearance and eloquence really did weigh on me! Not with difficulty then would I reply to them as Homer's Paris did to Hector:

> "In truth, the honored gifts of the gods are
> not to be scorned;
> whatever they bestow, no one would deny
> willingly." [*Apology* 4; *Iliad* 3.68–69]

Such contempt for one's enemies is clearly modeled on the *Apology* of Socrates with its proposal that a fine of only one mina be imposed (Plato, *Apology* 38B). According to the historian of the sophists, Philostratus, the sage Apollonius of Tyana recommended an attitude of insouciance on the part of anyone called upon to defend the intellectual life. Also, he advised, one would not be harmed by invoking the example of Socrates; the parallel would be flattering (*Apollonius of Tyana* 8.7).

The *Apology* requires about four hours to deliver, yet of the 114 pages in a modern text such as the Teubner edition of Rudolf Helm, scarcely half are devoted to refutations of specific charges. These proportions are not due to Apuleius' prolix style; they are signs that the speech is a clever piece of rhetorical *ethopoiia*, or characterization. Apuleius transforms a debate on the issues of a civil suit into an encomium of the philosopher's life. He becomes an African Socrates who appears to have only a detached, scientific interest in magic. As if reading from the driest of textbooks, he defines the word *magia* by a learned etymology based on a direct quotation in Greek from Plato's dialogue *Alcibiades I,* 125E:

The persons whom they call the royal tutors take charge of a boy when he is twice seven years of age; four are selected from the highest order of Persians as regarded by their age: the wisest, the most just, the most prudent, and the bravest. Of these, one teaches the magic of Zoroaster and Oromazes; he also teaches the art of kingship. [*Apology* 25]

Apuleius then continues by observing that magic is the art of worshiping the gods, something pious and holy; if that is a crime, no one would mind confessing to it, for to be a *magus* would be no more than to be a *sacerdos* or priest. Ignorant people frequently charge their intellectual superiors with practicing magic, it is said; Epicurus was called a magician simply because he studied the world with an insatiable curiosity, and Apuleius' ignorant prosecutors likewise mistake his curious investigations for the enchantments of a sorcerer. So runs the argument, with a scholarly squint on almost every page.

Now, not even the most bookish of scholars could entirely ignore magic's reputation as an evil science. Black magic is scarcely suited to the "wisest, the most just, the most prudent, and the bravest" of men, and Apuleius at last brings himself to admit as much:

This kind of magic, so far as I know about it, is something forbidden by law from early antiquity and the time of the Twelve Tables because it causes criminal barrenness of crops. For this reason it is occult and hidden, no less than loathesome and horrible: a thing usually guarded against by night, withdrawn into the shadows, isolated from control, murmured in verses, to which not only few slaves but also few free men are attracted. [*Apology* 47]

At every turn Apuleius suggests that he has no firsthand knowledge of black magic. When he does answer a specific allegation, he manages to give the impression that his heart is only in learning, as if he had come into the law courts directly from his study. In reply to the charge that he procured fish for a magical concoction, he protests that he was only studying fish anatomy, just like Aristotle or Theophrastus:

Now you cry out that I have learned magic words for an Egyptian or Babylonian rite: *selacheia, malaceia, malacostraca, chondracantha, ostracoderma, carcharodonta, amphibia, lepidōta, pholidōta, dermoptera, steganopoda, monērē, synagelastica.*[8] I could go still further, but it is not worthwhile wasting the day with things like this. I must go on to other things. [*Apology* 38]

To an ignorant or superstitious listener this recitation might well sound like a magic incantation. Compare the sound of the fish names to a genuine magic spell, such as occurs many times in the Greek magic papyri.[9] But in fact Apuleius is only a learned man reciting harmless Greek. We should scarcely expect him to do otherwise. A speech in *defense* against the charge of being a magician is the last place to search for revealing, intimate knowledge about magic.[10] The most Apuleius will ever admit is that his scientific and philosophical studies are susceptible to misinterpretation: Epicurus, Socrates, and other great thinkers had to contend with the prejudice of the ignorant, and now so does he. Here is an argument of innocence by association.

Apuleius was not the only sophist to face such annoying problems. Philostratus reports that one Adrian of Phoenicia, a pupil of Herodes Atticus who also lived in the second century, told so many tales about the marvelous deeds of magicians that he himself came to be regarded as one (*Lives of the Sophists* 590). Assuming that Apuleius won his case, it is tempting to speculate on the reasons he did so, other than the sheer justice of his plea. Perhaps it was Claudius' reluctance to rule against a man of such extensive learning; or perhaps it was Claudius' reward to Apuleius for one of the funniest orations ever delivered in a court of law.

8. Dogfish, molluscs, crustacea, dogfish with cartilaginous bones, flint skin, claw fish, amphibian fish, scale fish, scale snakes, bat fish, webfoots, solo fish, and school fish.

9. See the prayers to Typhon in Appendix 2.

10. Adam Abt, *Die Apologie des Apuleius von Madaura und die antike Zauberei* (Giessen, 1908), 332–335; for a detailed commentary revealing the highly rhetorical character of the speech, see H. E. Butler and A. S. Owen, *Apulei Apologia* (Oxford, 1914).

Apuleius employs an agglutinative kind of discourse that leaves no literary reference unused. The most amusing part of the speech comes when he answers the charge that he had once written some occasional verses on toothpaste. His prosecutors allege that this activity does not befit a serious man, but he explains the verses in the following manner. First we hear the offending poem:

> Calpurniane, salve properis versibus.
> misi, ut petisti, tibi munditias dentium,
> nitelas oris ex Arabicis frugibus,
> tenuem, candificum, nobilem pulvisculum,
> complanatorem tumidulae gingivulae,
> converritorem pridianae reliquiae,
> ne qua visatur tetra labes sordium,
> restrictis forte si labellis riseris.

> Calpurnius, greetings in hurried verses. I've sent some toothpaste to you, as you asked, brightener of the mouth from fruits of Arabia, fine, whitening, renowned powder, a soothing thing for the swollen little gum, a sweeper away of yesterday's scraps, so that no putrid blemish may be seen if by chance you expose your teeth in a laugh.   [*Apology* 6]

This *pièce d'occasion* is quite harmless, particularly when we compare it to Catullus' poem to Ignatius upon which it is based. To quote only its ending:

> nunc Celtiber es: Celtiberia in terra,
> quod quisque minxit, hoc sibi solet mane
> dentem atque russam defricare gingivam,
> ut quo iste vester expolitior dens est,
> hoc te amplius bibisse praedicet loti.

> Now you're from Spain, and Spain is the place where teeth are brushed and red gums rubbed with what is pissed into a pot the night before, so that the more polished your teeth are, the more they proclaim how greedily you've drunk your own piss. [Catullus, 39.17–21]

The topic is far from exhausted. We next learn from Apuleius that a clean mouth is essential to any philosopher's well-being. That advocacy of oral hygiene and a learned allusion to a common Homeric phrase, "the hedge of the teeth" (*Iliad* 4.350, *Odyssey* 1.64, etc.), produce this line of reasoning:

No doubt it is a crime not to be overlooked in a philosopher, if he is particularly precautious about dirt; if he allows no part of his body that is exposed to view to be unclean and filthy—the mouth especially, which man makes frequent use of openly and conspicuously, whether he kisses another or discourses on any subject or lectures before an audience or repeats his prayers in a temple. For so it is that words precede every act of mankind; words that, as the first of poets says, issue forth from the "hedge of the teeth." [*Apology* 7]

And why is the mouth so important to men? Some reflection is called for:

At all events, according to my way of thinking, I should say that nothing so ill becomes a man who is of free and liberal education as inattention to the appearance of his mouth. For this portion of the person is elevated in position, exposed to full view, and in continual use. On the other hand, with wild beasts and cattle the mouth is low-seated, and brought down on a level with the legs. It lies close to the feet and to the grass on which they feed and is scarcely ever to be seen but when they are dead or in a state of exasperation and ready to bite... whereas you look upon no feature before this one in a man while he is silent, and none more frequently while he is in the act of speaking. [*Apology* 7]

After turning aside his prosecutor's charge with the hope that Aemilianus will never use mouthwash (appropriately enough, considering the context)—"... Let his malignant tongue, the caterer of falsehoods and of bitter abuse, forever lie amid the stench and foulness that so well become it" (*Apology* 8)—Apuleius ends his defense of those by now forgotten verses on toothpaste with an observation that Mother Nature herself teaches men why their mouths should be clean:

But why enlarge any further upon this topic with regard to mankind? That huge beast, the crocodile, which is engendered in the Nile, even it, as I am informed, opens wide its jaws and without inflicting injury allows its teeth to be cleaned. For as it has an immense mouth and no tongue, and generally lies concealed beneath the water, numbers of leeches fasten about its teeth. Therefore it retires to the banks of the river, opens its mouth, and one of the river birds (its friend) thrusts in her beak and picks the teeth without incurring any risk. [*Apology* 8]

The argument—if that is the right word for all this—has soared away from Apuleius' harmless occasional poem, through Catullus, Homer, and animal husbandry, and has finally come to rest in the jaws of a crocodile. In a manner of speaking, so also has Aemilianus.

3

Yet the *Apology* is much more than a baroque variation of Platonic spirit and theme. It also reveals an important facet of Apuleius' development as a sophist—a second creative "life," apart from that as a novelist. To model one's own career on the exploits of heroes or sages was a familiar practice in antiquity. Odysseus, for example, was much esteemed by the Stoics for his ability to endure hardships, while Platonists valued him as an incarnation of practical wisdom, a paradigm for the contemplative life.[11] In writing *The Golden Ass*, Apuleius created his own version of the mythical adventures of Odysseus; in delivering the *Apology*, he obviously drew on the example of Socrates by making his trial a defense of the philosophical life before a court of public opinion. He was beguiled by the possibility of re-creating the glorious moments of Socrates' trial in 399 B.C.

We cannot be sure which of these two lives Apuleius lived first. But we can be reasonably certain that at his trial—the one crisis in his life about which we are well informed—and likewise in his supreme creative effort, he modeled himself on the portraits of Odysseus and Socrates in Greek literature. He himself makes the point. At the end of his treatise *On the God of Soc-*

11. For the way in which paradigmatic figures in literature became cultural models, see Jacques Bompaire, *Lucien écrivain: Imitation et création*, Bibliothèque des écoles francaises d'Athèns et de Rome, fasc. 190 (Paris, 1958), 13–98; W. B. Stanford, *The Ulysses Theme*, 2nd ed. (Oxford, 1963), 118–127; and F. Buffière, *Les mythes d'Homère et la pensée grecque* (Paris, 1956), 365–391.

rates, [12] Apuleius first lauds Socrates as a man deserving of his reputation solely on account of his own talents:

Then in similar fashion, in your scrutiny of men, do not reckon up extraneous things that do not belong to a man, but consider the man himself at the very core of his being, observe him in his poverty, like my Socrates. For I term things that do not belong to him those which his parents gave birth to and those which fortune bestowed. None of these would I add to my praise of Socrates: neither his birth nor his lineage nor his ancient ancestry nor enviable riches; for all of these are, as I have said, extraneous to him. It was glory for the son of Porthaon that he was such a man as not to shame his grandson. Thus you may reckon in similar fashion that all these qualities are extraneous to a man: "He is well born": you praise his parents. "He is rich": I do not trust fortune. I list only these ideas: "He is vigorous": he will grow weak in sickness; "he is handsome": wait a little while and he will not be. "Yes, but he is learned in the fine arts and in a superior way and, as much as is allowed a man, a connoisseur and a good counsel." At last finally you have praised the man himself! For this is not an inheritance from his father, nor does it depend on fortune, nor is it replaceable by the suffrage of the people, nor is it perishable with the body nor changeable with age. All these things does my Socrates possess, and that is why he disdains to have the others. [*On the God of Socrates* 23]

The parallel is easy enough to trace in the character of Lucius, who similarly discovered the essentials for a happy life. He found that a respectable family, good looks, and a successful career were of little help when blind Fortune turned against him. Recall the praise of his family and fortune at 3.11 and the remarks of the priest of Isis at 11.15: "Neither was your birth nor your high reputation, nor even that by which you flourish, your education, of any help."

The praise of Socrates leads directly to the conclusion of the work, which is a plea to the listener to imitate the life of Odysseus. We turn from contemplating the only true virtues to considering the qualities that enable a person to survive the vicissitudes of fortune. First, a long question:

Why then do you not also gird yourself for the pursuit of wisdom, indeed hurry to do so, so that you hear nothing said in praise of you

12. The "god" (*deus*) of the title is the "divine sign" or *daimonion sēmeion* of which Socrates speaks in Plato, *Apology* 31C–32A.

that does not belong to you, but rather that he who wishes to praise you would render you famous as Accius praised Ulysses in his *Philoctetes*, at the beginning of the tragedy: "Illustrious man, descended from a humble nation, of name renowned and powerful in your noble heart, founder of the Achaean fleet, avenger grievous to the Trojan people, son of Laertes"?

Then its interpretation:

The last thing he mentions is the name of his father. Well now, you have already heard the praises of Ulysses: there is nothing here that Laertes or Anticlia or Arcisius could claim for themselves. As you can see, the entire eulogy belongs to Ulysses. Nor is Homer's lesson about this man different in any way: he always wanted Prudence as Odysseus' companion, and, as poets will do, he named her Minerva. Thus, with this same companion, he approached all kinds of horrors, conquered all obstacles; with her aid he entered into the cave of the Cyclops, but came out again; he saw the cattle of the Sun, but refrained from touching them; he went down to Hades and made his way back; with that same wisdom as his companion he sailed past Scylla and was not kept prisoner; he drank the poison of Circe and was not transformed; he visited the Lotus Eaters and did not stay there; he heard the Sirens and did not approach them.   [*On the God of Socrates* 24]

Compare the conclusion of *On the God of Socrates* with the triumph of Lucius in Book 11: there, too, it was a goddess who delivered the hero from his misfortunes:

Yet even so, blind Fortune, while she tortured you with the worst dangers, has in her improvident malice brought you to this state of religious beatitude. Let her go now and rage with all her fury and seek some other object for her cruelty; for those people whose lives the majesty of our goddess has claimed for her service, for them dire calamity has no place. What gain did wicked Fortune derive from bandits, what from wild beasts, what from slavery, what from wandering here and there on the hardest of journies, what from the fear of death to which you were daily exposed?   [11.15]

In the *Apology*, the exemplary life of Socrates is realized with wit and immense vitality. In the same way the story of Lucius extends Apuleius' talents into a new yet related genre of literature. *The Golden Ass* is an odyssey for the soul of second-century man.

In light of the concluding lines of *On the God of Socrates,* the familiar polarity of seriousness and frivolity in Apuleius' work may more fruitfully be conceived of as the opposing examples of the lives of Socrates and Odysseus combined within the single artistic personality of Apuleius; yet, as we can also observe, these two lives are truly not opposites but complementary to one another. The Socratic life answers to our need to pursue transcendent ideals; the Odyssean, to satisfy our thirst for adventure, the fantastic, and the marvelous. Furthermore, Socrates is not to be equated simply with "seriousness" or Odysseus with "frivolity." We would do great injustice to Plato's portrait of Socrates if we did not bear in mind that that philosopher was as witty a man as ever lived. Invariably he approached a philosophical question with as much irony and unpredictability as the most entertaining novelist. Similarly, Odysseus possessed the trait that is basic to philosophy and to science—an overwhelming desire to know. He is the mythological paradigm of the philosopher and the scientist, as, for example, Daedalus is of the artist and the craftsman.

Apuleius' appraisal of Socrates and Odysseus is reflected in some of the most typical themes of *The Golden Ass* and the *Apology.* Individual talent and intellectual attainment are the qualities that most distinguish a man from all others, and of all qualities they are the most lasting. At the same time, one's desire for knowledge and one's thirst for new experiences must be tempered by prudence and caution. Curiosity may lead to all kinds of adventures, even to exaltation, but it requires an Athena—or an Isis—to ward off the dangers that invariably ensue. *On the God of Socrates* is an important text not only for its exposition of Plato's demonology but also for its epilogue. The treatise suggests that in Apuleius' view, combining the roles of philosopher and novelist made a great deal of sense.

4

Now that we have traced the outlines of Apuleius' career as novelist and philosopher, something further might be said about the nature of the second of these creative lives.

For Apuleius and for every literary artist of his day, success depended on expert use of the spoken word. As he once put it, only one theater exists, but in that theater an audience may hear anything, from frivolous entertainment to the most serious philosophical discourse:

For you have assembled with a good aim in this theater, knowing that the place does not detract from the authority of a speech delivered there. The main point to be considered is what you find in the theater. If it is a mime, you will laugh; if it is a tightrope walker, you will tremble; if it is a comedy, you will applaud; if it is a philosopher, you will learn. [*Florida* 5]

The *Florida*, an anthology of purple patches from his epideictic speeches, parallels perfectly the variety of diversions here described. The selections were most likely assembled by some connoisseur of Apuleian style rather than by the author himself. (It is hard to imagine that he could ever have brought himself to condense anything he had written.) No single principle for the selection or arrangement of the collection is apparent, save that every piece is diverting and clearly designed for public recitation.[13] The topics of the *Florida* reflect the same range as do the orations of Dio Chrysostom or Aelius Aristides: from India and the gymnosophists to Alexander the Great, from Hippias the Sophist to the parrot, from Crates the philosopher and his virgin bride, Hipparche, to Pythagoras and the island of Samos, to the amazing tale of the death of the comic poet Philemon. These are not the products of a genuinely philosophical mind, and the personality that emerges is far from austere. Apuleius' taste in rhetorical works corresponds with the Milesian taste he indulged in his novel. In both genres the didactic urge competes equally with the desire to entertain. Popularization and intellectual pretension distinguish all of Apuleius' surviving works.

The affinities between Apuleius the novelist and Apuleius the philosopher—the Socratic and the Odyssean paradigms—would probably be more apparent if the *Florida* were as familiar to us as *The Golden Ass* or the *Apology*. The kind of rhetoric found in the *Florida* does not appeal to modern tastes, and there

13. P. Vallette, *Apulée: Apologie, Florides,* 2d ed. (Paris, 1960), xxv-xxxi.

have been few translations. Yet the quickest way for any reader to become acquainted with the novelties of Apuleius' literary style is via the short pieces of the *Florida*. One sample is singled out for the present discussion: Apuleius' story of the Cynic philosopher Crates. The anecdote is presumably told to show that a vow of poverty can bring unexpected rewards:

When Crates had learned these things and others of this kind, partly from Diogenes, partly through his own efforts, at last he went forth into the forum, threw down his money like a load of dung—it was more a burden than an advantage—and when a crowd was assembled, he then exclaimed: "Crates emancipates Crates!" From that point on, he was not only alone but naked and free of everything. As long as he lived, he lived blessedly.

And so desirable was he that a noble virgin scorned her younger and richer suitors, and chose Crates for herself. Thereupon Crates took off his cloak and showed her that he was a hunchback. Then he put his purse and walking stick and cloak on the ground, and declared to the girl that what she saw there constituted his material possessions. And straightaway he advised her earnestly never afterward to find cause for a quarrel in anything that he had shown her. All the same, Hipparche accepted his terms. She replied that the subject had already been considered and pondered over quite long enough; she would never be able to find a richer or more handsome husband in all the world: he might lead her off wherever he pleased.

The Cynic led her into the portico, and there, in a heavily frequented spot, he lay down on her, in broad daylight, and would soon have openly deprived the maiden of her virginity—a thing she was ready to lose with indifference—had not Zeno blocked off the spectacle of his master from the circle of bystanders by holding up his tattered cloak. [*Florida* 14]

The moral of this anecdote is that Apuleius' listeners should learn to look beyond surface appearances to an underlying reality—to the kind of values that really matter. Hipparche exemplifies this virtue by her indifference to the poverty and deformity of her future husband; she is attracted to what is more important, his strong character. Of course the rather unexpected denouement on the floor of the portico goes somewhat beyond that simple lesson. Like the Milesian tales of *The Golden Ass*, this tale turns out to be entertaining in a bizarre way yet at the same time perfectly intelligible as an example of Cynic morality.[14]

The *Florida* also amply supports Apuleius' claim to being a polymath—an accomplishment, it will be recalled, he takes no pains to conceal in the *Apology*. Here is his description of his training as a sophist:

There is a well-known saying of a wise man about the table: the first cup is for thirst, the second for mirth, the third for joy, the fourth for madness. Concerning the goblet of the Muses, one might say the very opposite: the more often it is taken pure and unmixed, by that much more does it lead to soundness of mind. The first cup, from the schoolmaster, relieves the spirit; the second, from the grammarian, forms learning; the third, from the rhetorician, arms one with eloquence. Up to this point many have drunk. But *I* have drunk from other goblets at Athens: the inventive cup of poetry, the limpid one of geometry, the sweet one of music, the rather austere one of dialectic, and above all the cup of universal philosophy—inexhaustible and nectareous. For Empedocles composes poems; Plato, dialogues; Socrates, hymns; Epicharmus, mimes; Xenophon, histories; Crates, satires; your Apuleius embraces all these genres and cultivates the nine Muses with equal zeal. And if he does so with obviously greater goodwill than talent, for that very reason perhaps is he all the more to be praised.

In every good action it is the effort that is meritorious; the outcome is a matter of chance. And likewise in the case of a bad deed, a criminal intent, even when it is not realized, falls under the penalty of law: the soul is stained with blood, the hand remains pure. Therefore just as it is enough to merit punishment if one only thinks about a crime, so also is it enough grounds for praise if one only attempts a good deed.

What greater praise could one merit, what more substantial, than in speaking well of Carthage, where you, an entire city, are the most cultivated of men, who have in your possession all learning, which your children learn, your young men display, your old ones teach? Carthage, the venerable schoolmistress of our province, Carthage the heavenly Muse of Africa, Carthage, Camena[15] to the people who wear the toga! [*Florida* 20]

14. A biographical sketch of Crates is also the theme of *Florida* 22. The Cynics specialized in repulsive but improving displays of this sort; see Donald R. Dudley, *A History of Cynicism* (London, 1937), 44–53.
15. The Latin word for Muse.

Never mind that overflowing cup. The varied roles of philosopher, poet, naturalist, historian, and grammarian are only so many poses designed to enhance the image of Apuleius the orator: to every audience he was a source of boundless culture and learning. In all his writing Apuleius is, like Lucius, the center of attention; his is a virtuoso's temperament, and his works are an expression of that temperament.

From his stay in the Greek cities of the Roman Empire, and perhaps also in such a center of learning as Carthage, Apuleius learned to direct his literary and oratorical talents along a particular course—one less familiar to the Latin-speaking western parts of the Empire, perhaps, but quite recognizable in the east.[16] The themes of Apuleius' works are similar to the lectures (*dialexeis*) of such Greek sophists as Maximus of Tyre, who declaimed at Rome during the reign of Commodus (A.D. 180–192). Maximus spoke on such topics as "What was the *daimōn* of Socrates?" (*Lectures* 8–9) and "Which is the better life: theoretical or practical?" (*Lectures* 15–16); both sides of each topic were argued with equal conviction. For his part, Apuleius seems to have been quite adept in the skill that artists and intellectuals through the ages have had to practice to make their way— teaching. He usually is to be found informing someone of something—even in a story such as that of Crates and Hipparche. It is this didacticism that makes his philosophy seem more suited to the lecture room or the theater than to the solitary confines of the philosopher's study. Apuleius was a virtuoso, a verbal concert artist; thus his works invariably succeed in calling as much attention to the performer as to the merits of the work performed.

The circumstances of performance inevitably affected the character of the literature Apuleius turned out. Anyone who has ever lectured for a fee, no matter how small, will perhaps appreciate the exhilaration that comes with speaking for money. On such occasions it is tempting to say what one imagines will please one's listeners, not annoy them; individuals determined

16. Apuleius' education in Greece is mentioned in *Florida* 18; see translation in Appendix 1.

to speak only the truth as they see it may do so, to be sure, but they will not always excel in making a living. Fortunately for Apuleius, the truth as he perceived it appears to have been what his audiences wished to hear. In fact, his audiences seemed ready to hear whatever he had to say.

This aspect of the sophist's profession was later idealized by the biographer Philostratus:

> When a certain one of the quibblers enquired why he asked no questions, Apollonius replied, "Because when I was a boy I asked questions; there is no need for me to ask questions now, but rather to teach the things I have discovered."
>
> "How, then, Apollonius, will a wise man discourse?" asked the other yet again.
>
> "Like a lawgiver," he said, "for the lawgiver should deliver to the many those instructions about which he has persuaded himself."
>
> In this way he pursued matters while in Antioch and converted to himself the most unrefined people. [*Apollonius of Tyana* 1.17]

If the sophists were highly esteemed by their audiences, that devotion was amply repaid. Like Aelius Aristides, Apuleius was proud of his provincial origins and took special delight in appearing before the citizens of Carthage, his "teachers, nurses, parents, whose name I praise wherever I go" (*Florida* 18).[17] Aristides also experienced a lengthy conversion to the healing god Asclepius.[18] Conversion to belief in some kind of transcendent authority was a familiar occurrence in the lives of sophists in the Roman Empire. Apuleius, Aristides, and others made these intensely private experiences a matter of public record through their art.

Dio Chrysostom ("Dio of the golden mouth"), of an earlier generation than Apuleius, experienced a gradual conversion to philosophy from his first love, rhetoric. He was seeking a sys-

17. Cf. Aristides, *Monody for Smyrna* (*Oration* 18). Philostratus says that when Aristides came to the words "West winds blow through the desert city," the emperor Marcus Aurelius wept and resolved at once to help rebuild the town, which had suffered an earthquake (*Lives of the Sophists* 582). The sentiment loses some of its power when read in isolation.

18. C. A. Behr, *Aelius Aristides and the Sacred Tales* (Chicago, 1969), 23–40.

tem of values that would make life more tolerable; philosophy provided a means of escape from a life of luxury, self-indulgence, and superstition. An oration delivered at Athens describes the eventual benefits that Dio gained through his banishment by the emperor Domitian. In the course of his exile he had ample opportunity to observe people in all their varied ways and soon reached the conclusion that the majority were fools. Some people called him a beggar or a tramp, others a philosopher. He appears to have acquired this last title with remarkably little effort, largely through the force of circumstance:

> For many of my questioners would approach me and ask what I thought about good and evil. The result was that I was forced to think about these matters so that I could answer my questioners. They would ask me to come back again and speak before the public. Accordingly it became necessary for me to speak also about the duties of men and about the things that seemed to me likely to profit them. [*Discourses* 13.12–13]

Dio goes on to tell of his efforts to avoid the vainglorious style of certain philosophers who were given to advertising themselves like Olympian heralds proclaiming the victors.

Apuleius felt no such urge toward reticence. His career reflects none of the struggles Dio went through. He experienced no difficulty at all in being simultaneously rhetorician and philosopher, despite his master Plato's vigorous criticism of rhetoricians' claims that their profession was an art (*technē*). In the *Gorgias* (463 B–C), for example, rhetoric is said to flatter the intellect in the same way that the talents of a cook flatter the palate. Plato's high standing among later students of rhetoric was not significantly harmed by this or any other of his criticisms of the art (especially in the *Phaedrus*). His style was so elegant they could not ignore him. Aristotle later showed that both rhetoric and philosophy were essential for any educated person (*Rhetoric* 1354A), and such Romans as Cicero shared this view (*On the Orator* 3.15–19); there should ideally be a wondrous association (*mirifica societas*) between the two. Despite such reasonable compromises, the rivalry between rhetoric and philosophy never ceased to provide a fertile topic for polemic. Isocrates, a contemporary of Plato and a figure of considerable importance in the history of education in antiquity, argued that philosophy was not the exclusive preserve of Socrates and his disciples merely because they had acted as if it were (*Antidosis* 270). Five hundred years after the death of Plato, Aelius Aristides, in his orations *To Plato* and *On the Four*, even went so far as to attempt to show that Plato did not really say what he appeared to be saying in the *Gorgias* and *Phaedrus*.[19]

In Apuleius' estimation, philosophy enjoyed a status little different from that of religion itself; it offered a means of making sense of an unpredictable and cruel world. Untroubled by Socrates' criticisms of rhetoric, Apuleius was free to treat philosophical works like sacred texts; great philosophers were *divini auctores*, divine beings.[20] The prime requirement for philosophical man was *fides*, faith, and *fides* is both Lucius' abiding characteristic throughout his travels and the reason for his conversion in Book 11. If such a deity as Isis offered hope of personal salvation (*spes salutis*), she required complete devotion in return. *Fides* confirmed the tie between god and man. If one were religious by nature, he could even participate in more than one religion. Apuleius did so; as proof he tells of carrying a figurine of one anonymous god about with him on his travels: "Cornelius Saturnius the artisan made for me a statue of whatever god he desired, whom I then worshiped as was my custom. He made it of whatever materials he had at hand: in this case, of wood" (*Apology* 61). The point of this anecdote is to show that he is pious and incapable of the deceit that magicians practiced: "For I have the habit wherever I am of carrying an image of some god amongst my books. I worship it on festival days with incense and wine, and sometimes even with a sacrifice" (*Apol-*

19. Aelius Aristides, *Orations* 45 and 46. The "four" of the second title are the Athenian statesmen Miltiades, Themistocles, Cimon, and Pericles, all of whom enjoyed flourishing careers without being philosophers. Aristides' hostility to philosophy is discussed in André Boulanger, *Aelius Aristide et la sophistique dans la province d'Asie au IIe siècle de notre ère* (Paris, 1923), 218–270.
20. Phillip De Lacy, "Plato and the Intellectual Life of the Second Century A.D.," in *Approaches to the Second Sophistic*, ed. G. W. Bowersock (University Park, Pa., 1974), 4–10; Ludwig Bieler, *Theios Anēr: Das Bild des "Göttlichen Menschen" in Spätantike und Frühchristentum* (Vienna, 1935–1936).

ogy 63). Notice that this piety is not only energetic but quite indiscriminate. He worships "an image of whichever god Cornelius desired"; faith comes first, then the object of that faith. For Apuleius and his contemporaries, *fides* provided a means of escape from what was for many an overwhelming feeling of personal vulnerability.[21]

5

Perhaps we can now better understand Apuleius' frequent allusions to Plato's dialogues, with every trace of the Socratic method and dialectic removed and without a hint of critical thought on the doctrines of Socrates. It is easy enough to see that he was not a philosopher in the true sense of the word. His most "philosophical" treatise is the one already drawn on in tracing his intellectual and creative ambitions. As a piece of rhetoric, *On the God of Socrates* is undeniably effective. It could make even the dullest audience aware of the nature of Socrates' *daimōn*.[22] But the powers of reasoning the treatise demands are minimal; allowance is even made for a limited attention span. There is no point in exaggerating Apuleius' philosophical acumen. His orations and treatises could be an important source of learning for those who had no access to the original Greek of Plato and the other philosophers; as we have seen, he was important to Augustine for this reason. But today we would no more think of trying to learn Plato's philosophy through Apuleius than of trying to study Newtonian physics via the heroic couplets of Alexander Pope. Such an undertaking might just be possible, but why would any sensible person wish to attempt it?

Yet it would be unfair to end our appraisal of Apuleius the philosopher on a negative note. He was not interested in pursuing the kind of critical work in philosophy that would have

21. E. R. Dodds, *Pagan and Christian in an Age of Anxiety* (Cambridge, 1965), 37–68.

22. *On the God of Socrates* is the most extensive treatise on *daimones* that we have from classical antiquity; for demonology before Apuleius, see Jean Beaujeu, *Apulée: Opuscules philosophiques* (Paris, 1973), 183–201.

earned him more praise today.[23] But then, why should he have been? A disciple of the sophistic, a man secure in the knowledge that he could investigate the inner workings of the cosmos, Apuleius had no special call to force dialectic or the more difficult problems of metaphysics on the attention of any audience. More important was that he persuade his listeners to believe what he was saying: *he* already knew the truth. In this regard, his approach was the very opposite of that of his master Socrates, who on all occasions professed to know nothing and to have only questions, not answers—to the eternal annoyance of many who heard him (Plato, *Apology* 23A–24B).

Apuleius devoted his energies to the way in which he expressed his ideas. A typical example of his philosophizing oratory comes near the beginning of *On the God of Socrates*, in a long sentence describing the mixture of good and evil that characterizes the human condition. If that idea is scarcely novel, Apuleius' way of expressing it is another matter:[24]

And so men—possessing the gift of speech; waxing in reason; with immortal spirits; with dying limbs; with light and fretful minds; with brutish and loathsome bodies; with dissimilar characters; similar errors; with presumptuous audacity; tenacious hopes; empty fortune; taken singly, mortal; yet altogether as a single race, immortal; changing places in turn with an offspring to take their place; with a brief space of time; with sluggish understanding; with a swift death; with a life filled with complaint—dwell on earth.

igitur homines ratione plaudentes, oratione pollentes, immortalibus animis, moribundis membris, levibus et anxiis mentibus, brutis et obnoxiis corporibus, dissimillimis moribus, similibus erroribus, pervicaci

23. Opinion has long been divided about the authenticity of Apuleius' other philosophical works: *On the Doctrine of Plato* is a rapid and dull survey of Plato's life and ethical teachings, *On the Cosmos* is a treatise based on a work falsely attributed to Aristotle, and *On Interpretation* is an exposition in Greek of Aristotelean logic. All three works are now generally accepted as being by Apuleius, though their style and language are quite plain and arid compared to those of *The Golden Ass*, the *Apology*, and the *Florida*.

24. Augustine quotes the entire sentence but is himself so attuned to the florid Latin style that he makes no mention of the passage's rhetorical qualities (*On the City of God* 9.8).

audacia, pertinaci spe, casso labore, fortuna caduca, singillatim
mortales, cunctim tamen universo genere perpetui, vicissim sufficienda
prole mutabiles, volucri tempore, tarda sapientia, cita morte, querula
vita, terras incolunt. [*On the God of Socrates* 4]

Even if we recognize that Apuleius is here employing the rhetorical figure of *peribolē,* or *circumducta oratio* (fullness of expression, amplification of an idea), it is hard to see the reason for
such prolixity. The idea of human mortality is spun out in endless ornamentation, like the slow movement in a particularly
dull set of rococo variations. But let the sentence be arranged to
show the aural effects, and it is clear at once that Apuleius was
interested as much in the sounds of the words as in their meaning:

> igitur homines
>
> > *ratione plaudentes,*
> > *oratione pollentes,*
> >
> > immortalibus anim*is,*
> > moribundis membr*is,*
> >
> > levibus et an*xiis* ment*ibus,*
> > brutis et obno*xiis* corpor*ibus,*
> >
> > *dissimil*limis mor*ibus,*
> > *simil*ibus error*ibus,*
> >
> > *per*vica*ci* audacia,
> > *per*tina*ci* spe,
> >
> > casso labore,
> > fortuna caduca,
> >
> > *singillatim* mortal*es,*
> > *cunctim* tamen universo genere perpetui,
> > *vicissim* sufficienda prole mutabil*es,*
> >
> > volucri tempore,
> > tarda sapientia,
> >
> > cita morte,
> > querula vita,
> >
> > > terras incolunt.

The rhetorical figures of the sentence are achieved as follows: The basic idea, that men dwell on the earth (*igitur homines... terras incolunt*), surrounds an elaborate series of paired phrases, most of which are in the ablative case. Many words are juxtaposed to underscore the opposition of antithetical ideas, as in "immortal" and "dying" (*immortalibus, moribundis*), or "minds" and "bodies" (*mentibus, corporibus*). The rhymes, or *homoeoteleuta*, are comparatively easy to achieve in such an inflected language as Latin; for example, the couplets using -*es*, -*is*, and -*ibus* and the quatrains using -*e* and -*a* arranged in a pattern of -*a* -*e* -*e* -*a* and -*e* -*a* -*e* -*a*. Further elegances abound: the word "reason" is changed to "speech" by the addition of the letter *o* (*ratio, oratio*); the prefix *dis*- is removed to change the adjective "dissimilar" into "similar"; the intensifying prefix *per*- ("thoroughly") is twice used; and the three adverbs "singly," "altogether," and "in turn" are grouped to achieve the rhyme of -*im* (*singillatim, cunctim, vicissim*). These figures of speech both complement and shape the thought; the uncertain, ever changing state of affairs in our daily lives is perfectly represented by the ever changing forms of the words. Even a brief exposition of the passage's artifices reveals the source of its immediate appeal. The most salient features of this style—rhyme, puns, antitheses, and balanced, rhythmical phrases—could be grasped easily at first hearing. A simple idea is presented, and rhetoric, not philosophy, has played the major role in shaping it. We should expect no less from literature of the second century.[25]

Apuleius' language should be of interest to every curious reader of *The Golden Ass*. His career as a "philosopher" was as successful as that of any other literary artist known to posterity; save for the cause célèbre of his trial on a charge of practicing black magic, it was just as conventional. *The Golden Ass*, like

25. If a lexicographer can be any guide in these matters, philosophy may not even have received its tithe. When the sophist Julius Pollux compiled an *onomasticon* or glossary ca. 166–176, he devoted eleven times as much space in it to the entries *rhētōr* and *sophistēs* as he did to *philosophus* (a concept evidently of far less interest); see Erich Bethe, *Pollucis Onomasticon* (Leipzig, 1900), vol. 1, 208–216.

everything else Apuleius wrote, was intended to appeal to the prevailing literary tastes of the second century. It was written to please the ears of an audience whose regular fare was provided by those concert artists of the spoken word, the sophists of the Roman Empire.

CHAPTER 5

The Language of
a Sophist's Novel

For who of you would forgive me a single mistake in grammar? Who would acquit me of one syllable's mispronunciation? Who would permit me rashly to blabber out rude and corrupt words as they occurred, like a madman? These are things you easily pardon in others—and rightly so—but you scrutinize closely every single thing I say; you weigh it out with a fine measure; you test it with a file and rule; you check its smoothness by the lathe and its seriousness by the buskin of tragedy. Modest accomplishment meets with as much excuse as genuine merit meets with difficulty. So do I acknowledge my difficulty: I ask nothing but that you examine me in this way.

—Apuleius to an audience of
Carthaginians (*Florida* 9)

1

"THE END": such is A. D. Leeman's assessment of the abject state of letters in the second century.

Since the times of the Humanists it has been usual to call the first century B.C. that of the *Aurea Latinitas,* and the first century A.D. that of the *Argentea Latinitas.* Pursuing the same imagery we could call the second century that of the *Aenea Latinitas*—'*Tertia post illa successit aenea proles.*' But Ovid's next line, *Saevior ingeniis et ad horrida promptior arma,* surely does not apply. The bronze of this age rather suggests the old-world patina of the Corinthian bronzes, exhibited by industrious collec-

tors in art galleries, in which an unreal and somewhat dusty peaceful-
ness reigned supreme.[1]

Our survey of Apuleius' activities as stylist and orator brings us
toward the end of this literary study—though perhaps not quite
the sort of end Leeman has described. Apuleius expected his
listeners to pay attention not only to the substance of his prose
but to its wording and style.

A good deal of his time and effort was devoted to matters that
few of his present-day readers are likely to care much about.
Most literary criticism of *The Golden Ass* has either ignored its
extraordinary style and language or mentioned them only in
passing—sometimes with barely concealed distaste. The language and style have of course attracted considerable separate
study, in which the relevance of Apuleius' highly artificial language to the interpretation of the novel has been left aside.[2] For
studies in the history of Latin, that is understandable; but to
divide forever literary exegesis from any consideration of
Apuleius' language will not in the long run improve our understanding of the novel. As readers move through Lucius' tales,
they will surely realize that they are confronted time and again
with rhetorical set pieces—very often in the most obvious form,
that of a speech. But sometimes the sophist's art manifests itself
in such less familiar devices as the *ecphrasis* or ornately descriptive passage on Actaeon (2.4) and the encomium on women's
hair inspired by Fotis (2.7–10); and sometimes the narrative
pauses and becomes fixed on only the sounds of words. In fact,
the sophist's arts made a decisive impression on the texture of
Apuleius' prose. To appreciate the point, let us consider from a
somewhat broader perspective what it meant for Apuleius to
apply the arts of the sophist to his writing of *The Golden Ass*.

1. A. D. Leeman, *Orationis ratio: The Stylistic Theories and Practice of the Roman
Orators, Historians, and Philosophers* (Amsterdam, 1963), 364. He is quoting
Ovid's myth of the four races of man; see *Metamorphoses* 1.125–126: "After that
came a third race of bronze, of fiercer disposition and readier to take up savage
arms."

2. The major studies are Max Bernhard, *Der Stil des Apuleius von Madaura: Ein
Beitrag zur Stilistik des Spätlateins* (Stuttgart, 1927); Pierre Médan, *La latinité
d'Apulée dans les Métamorphoses* (Paris, 1926); and Louis Callebat, *Sermo cotidianus
dans les Métamorphoses d'Apulée* (Paris, 1968).

2

All ancient literature was to some extent aural, written as much for the ear as for the intellect.[3] As Quintilian observed, one need not be an advanced student of rhetoric to appreciate this point:

The best judge of artistic structure is the ear. It perceives fullness of rhythm, senses lack of it; is offended by unevenness, soothed by smoothness, excited by energetic movement; approves stability, detects limping measures, and rejects those that are excessive and extravagant. For these reasons those people who are trained understand the theory of artistic structure, and even the untrained derive pleasure from it. [*The Education of the Orator* 9.4.116]

The tutor of Pliny reminds us of the importance of listening in determining tasteful, effective prose style. We may be sure he would not have approved of the turn taken by certain stylists in the second century—notably by Apuleius, in the *prosa poetica* of *The Golden Ass.* Quintilian regarded the sound of versified prose as excessively ugly, *multo foedissimum* (9.4.72). This view was held also by Cicero (*Orator* 189) and by Aristotle (*Rhetoric* 1408B—1409A). Yet any rhetorician would have appreciated the purpose of Apuleius' unusual language: a work of literature had to be composed as much for the ear as for the critical intelligence of the listener.

For these reasons ancient rhetoricians were inclined to be precise in their analysis of a sentence.[4] A label and an appropriate usage existed for every choice of word, phrase, or clause, for every kind of rhythm, and for the sound effects that could be created by words. Such arrangements are hard to reproduce in English. Greek and Latin permit much greater freedom in the ordering of words than English allows. Scarcely a sentence was

3. This aspect of classical literature is perhaps not generally known to contemporary, "silent" readers; see W. B. Stanford, *The Sounds of Greek: Studies in Greek Theory and Practice of Euphony* (Berkeley, 1967).

4. A comprehensive survey of the history of rhetoric from its beginnings to later antiquity may be found in George Kennedy, *The Art of Persuasion in Greece* (Princeton, N.J., 1963), and *The Art of Rhetoric in the Roman World* (Princeton, N.J., 1972).

composed in which the choice of words, their order, and the rhythm produced were not given the closest attention.[5] Free word order may cause beginning students of Latin or Greek some memorable difficulties; yet, as the Greek rhetorician Dionysius of Halicarnassus explained, it was a desire for beauty, not obscurity, that led to such elaborate arrangement of words.[6] Quintilian explains what an author was attempting to achieve through this unending transposition:

> For our language would often be harsh, rough, limp, or disjointed, if the words were always arranged in their natural order and attached each to the other as they occur, despite the fact that there is no real bond of union. Consequently some words require postponement, others anticipation, with each being set in its proper place. For we are like those who build a wall of unhewn stone: we cannot hew or polish our words in order to make them fit more compactly, and so we must take them as they are and choose suitable positions for them. [*The Education of the Orator* 8.6.62]

To illustrate this search for words he tells an anecdote about Plato, who is said to have rearranged over and over on a wax tablet the opening four words of the *Republic*. Usually translated as "I went down yesterday to the Piraeus," the English word order happens to correspond with the Greek (*katebēn chthes eis Peiraia*), but this is quite accidental. With only slight resulting variations in emphasis, Plato could as well have written *chthes katebēn eis Peiraia* or *chthes eis Peiraia katebēn*. According to Quintilian, Plato decided on the final order because he found most pleasing the rhythm ⏑⏑–⏑–––– (in this scheme and all the following ones, ⏑ = a short syllable and – = a long syllable, equivalent to two ⏑⏑):

kă-tĕ-bēn chthĕs eīs Peī-raī-ā,

which was more attractive to the ear than

chthēs kă-tĕ-bēn eīs Peī-raī-ā

5. See L. R. Palmer, *The Latin Language* (London, 1961), 148–180.
6. D. A. Russell and M. Winterbottom, *Ancient Literary Criticism: The Principal Texts in New Translations* (Oxford, 1972), 321–343.

or

chthĕs eĩs Pei-rai-ā kă-tĕ-bēn.

To take only one example of this concern for elegant sound from Quintilian's own language, consider the care with which Cicero opens his *First Oration against Catiline:* the words are famous for their indignation; perhaps less widely appreciated is their studied variation of rhythm and sentence structure:

How long will you abuse our patience, Catiline? How much longer will this madness of yours make sport of us? To what limit will your unbridled boldness hurl itself? [*Against Catiline* 1.1]

So indignant is Cicero that he might for once have been expected to throw aside all attention to balance, antithesis, and the other niceties of style; but rhetoric is in fact as much in evidence as ever:

quo usque tandem	abutere,	Catilina,	patientia nostra?
quam diu etiam	furor iste tuus	nos	eludet?
quem ad finem	sese	effrenata	iactabit	audacia?

That is,

adverbial phrase	verb	subject	object
adverbial phrase	subject	object	verb
adverbial phrase	object	verb	subject.

Scarcely a page of any classical prose author survives that does not reveal such artistry to some degree. Orators, historians, and philosophers alike wrote with varying but rarely concealed interest in the arrangement and sound of their words, so that Quintilian's image of prose stylists as a fraternity of stonemasons is only the truth felicitously told.

3

In every human endeavor, even in the matter of prose style, some regard for the Golden Mean is desirable. Of course it was not observed. Contemporaneously with the historian Herodotus appeared writers who were quite happy to spend more time on the adornment than on the substance of their sentences. The best-known culprit was Gorgias of Leontini (fl. 427 B.C.). Even the fragments of his work that have come down to us constitute a perverse ideal whose spirit has reappeared from time to time since the fifth century B.C. One such time was the second century A.D. Many Greek and Latin stylists shared his peculiar way of looking at a sentence.[7] Of all Latin prose stylists, Apuleius was the most enamored of rhyme, *isocolon* (equal number of syllables), and antithesis. He is clearly a writer after Gorgias' spirit.

A surviving fragment of a funeral oration (*epitaphios*) provides some indication of Gorgias' prose style. One wonders what feelings were stirred up in the hearts of the grieving audience to whom the oration was addressed. In the concluding sentence of the fragment, Gorgias, striving after extremes of antithesis, juxtaposes such sharply contradictory ideas that the effect is impossible to reproduce in English without turning language into gibberish. Yet the words have such a bewitching sound that for a moment one almost forgets they were spoken at a state funeral:

Therefore now since they have died the longing for them does not die with them, but immortal in their not immortal bodies lives on after them who no longer live.   [*Funeral Oration*, frag.]

Still more literally:

toigaroun *autōn apothanontōn* ("therefore these having died")

ho pothos *ou synapethanen* ("the longing does not die with them")

all' *athanatos* ("but immortal," modifying *pothos*)

ouk en *anthanatois* sōmasi ("not in immortal bodies")

zei ("lives")

ou zōntōn ("of those not living")

7. "Sicily produced Gorgias of Leontini, and we must consider that the art of the sophists reaches back to him as though to its father" (Philostratus, *The Lives of the Sophists* 492). Plato gives us a delightful parody of Gorgias' style in the speech of the poet Agathon; see *Symposium* 194E–197E.

It is a remarkable elaboration on the observation "We are sorry to see them dead." Meaning is turned inside out: "immortal longing" for "not immortal bodies"; the words buzz and hum with a grief that "lives" for those "who do not live" (*zei ou zōntōn*). With as many subtleties as these on his mind, some have found it a wonder that Gorgias' writing achieves any meaning at all.[8]

As we may infer from the sentence near the beginning of *On the God of Socrates*, which was analyzed in Chapter 4, the spirit of Gorgias lived anew in Apuleius' prose style; the two are among the most poetic and magical of prose authors in their respective languages.[9] The utterances of Apuleius had to be not merely eloquent and effective but stunningly so. In this regard it is useful to compare Apuleius' literary compositions with the musical works of such a composer as Franz Liszt. In Liszt's works one likewise finds musical ideas cast into technically forbidding display pieces. The virtuosity is integral to Liszt's style, but it often strikes the unsympathetic listener as being so strong as to overwhelm the musical content. Similarly, to see Apuleius as merely a lecturer and a source of learning (which of course he was) is to see only part of the picture. His arts are fully realized only in performance—one might even go so far as to say, only in his personal performance. For a virtuoso's aim is to magnify and enhance his own personality through art; the performer becomes at least as important as the work he performs—as is perfectly illustrated by Apuleius' *Florida*.[10] Literary and musical virtuosity have their limitations, of course. If one is moved by the display, well and good; if not—and many modern readers are not moved by the euphuistic style of the Second Sophistic—such virtuosity may cause as much irritation as pleasure.

To what we may thus term a "Gorgianic strain" in his style,

8. See J. D. Denniston, *Greek Prose Style* (Oxford, 1945), 12: "Starting with the initial advantage of having nothing in particular to say, he was able to concentrate all his energies upon saying it."

9. Karl Polheim, *Die lateinische Reimprosa*, 2d ed. (Berlin, 1925), 133–157, 206. See also Jacqueline de Romilly, *Magic and Rhetoric in Ancient Greece* (Cambridge, Mass., 1975), 1–22.

10. See the translations of *Florida* 9 and 16 in Appendix 1.

Apuleius added a further preoccupation—an archaizing taste that led him to rummage through early Latin authors in search of old-fashioned words. This preoccupation was one he shared with most Latin authors of the second and third centuries.

The arbiter of all such archaic stylists was Marcus Cornelius Fronto (died ca. A.D. 166). He too was an African, and a tutor in rhetoric to members of the imperial family.[11] His most famous pupil was the future emperor Marcus Aurelius. Fronto is known to us mainly through his correspondence with Marcus, Lucius Verus, and other figures of the imperial court of the Antonines. These collections of letters testify to the supremacy of rhetoric in education—in Fronto's opinion, a supremacy well deserved. His correspondence reveals a horrifying enthusiasm for all aspects of rhetoric, particularly for the search for archaic words. Fronto was fascinated by the rich vocabulary of Ennius, Cato the Elder, and Plautus; his preoccupations with style, in turn, were shared by Apuleius, Aulus Gellius, Tertullian, and even later writers.[12] His letters also reveal something we can only infer from Apuleius' finished speeches: the hard work involved in searching for the right word. That task was unremitting, always exciting.

So devoted was Fronto to his beloved rhetoric that he had little use for the prolonged study of philosophy; it seems to have served him mainly as a useful propaedeutic for the higher calling of oratory. What he has to say about the discipline betrays little deep understanding of it. Criticisms can be relied on to turn on matters of style. To write in the words of the dialecticians would be to write of "a Jove who sighed, even wheezed, but did not thunder. Prepare instead a speech that is worthy of the meaning you draw from philosophy: the more nobly you feel, the more subtly will you speak" (*To Marcus Antoninus, On Elo-*

11. See M. Dorothy Brock, *Studies in Fronto and His Age* (Cambridge, 1911). Because Fronto, Apuleius, and others came from North Africa, the theory once was held that a separate dialect of "African Latin" existed; in fact, these authors had a common view of rhetoric and literary taste, not a common dialect, and they were following the example of Greek rhetoricians. See Eduard Norden, *Die Antike Kunstprosa* (Berlin, 1915), 1.344–392.

12. For the antiquarian tastes of Gellius' circle, see Barry Baldwin, *Studies in Aulus Gellius* (Lawrence, Kans., 1975).

quence 2.19). Philosophy by itself could not be trusted to produce *eloquentia,* the mastery of diction that was the goal of any serious orator. As Fronto put it in a letter to Marcus, it was better to avoid rhetoric altogether than have only a taste with the tip of the lips; for ineptitude in the choice and arrangement of words could be detected more easily than could ignorance in any other kind of art (*Letters to Marcus Antoninus* 4.3.1). We might compare this caution with the cup Apuleius manages to down in *Florida* 20.[13]

It is an irony of history that Fronto lost at least one battle to keep his pupils safely in rhetoric's camp. His most famous student ultimately turned toward an austere—even bleak—Stoicism; early in the *Meditations* Marcus even expresses relief at having learned to eschew excessive devotion to rhetoric, poetry, and "fine writing" (*Meditations* 1.17)—the very arts with which this chapter is concerned.

Aside from proselytizing for rhetoric, Fronto liked to explain the routine work required for the attainment of *eloquentia.* His vision of a correct style of Latin was derived from books, and it set a premium on the choice and arrangement of words. He explains to Marcus that a great variety of words was available, much as if one were choosing fruits or vegetables in some lexicographical market: ". . . weighty aphorisms from orators of old or sweet ones from poems or lustrous ones from history or affable ones from comedy or sophisticated ones from the Roman farces or charming and witty ones from the Atellane farces" (*Letters to Marcus Antoninus* 2.2).

So great was Fronto's love for unexpected and rare words that their mere absence in Cicero became grounds for criticism. Cicero, for all that he had been the "head and fountain of Roman eloquence" (*caput atque fons Romanae facundiae*), had not searched out words with proper care. He used words correctly, but he rarely startled his reader with an unexpected archaism; the aspiring orator would, alas, rarely find a source of unusual words in the works of Cicero (*Letters to Marcus Antoninus* 4.3.4). Even Roman history could be treated in terms of literary style, as

13. *Florida* 20 is quoted in Chapter 4.

Fronto shows in his comment on the so-called Year of the Four Emperors and other embarrassments of the imperial succession:[14] "The emperors, however, from that point onward to Vespasian, were all of the same type: one that causes no less shame for their words than regret for their morals and pity for their wrongs" (*Letters to Lucius Verus* 2.1.8). Most of Fronto's letters are not concerned to rise even to this level of historical acumen but are content to discuss spelling and the vexing choice of a new word over an older one. At all events, life afforded few pleasures greater than the recovery of rare old words. Anyone with an inherent agility of mind required only the "shining light of words" to attain artistic perfection. The orator's tasks were to find the right words, to put them in the right order, and to give them the right touch of antique style (*To Marcus Antoninus, On Eloquence* 2.1–4).

Although Fronto's standing suffered some decline when his letters were rediscovered in the early nineteenth century,[15] he had a considerable reputation in antiquity. Unquestionably artists in his lifetime and long afterward found a spokesman in him. In the generation after Apuleius, Tertullian continued the tradition of the florid style of the *Florida* and *The Golden Ass*. Tertullian's concern for rare and dazzling words would surely have earned Fronto's praise:

mutant et bestiae pro veste formam; quamquam et pavo pluma vestis, et quidem de cataclistis, immo omni conchylio pressior qua colla florent, et omni patagio inauratior qua terga fulgent, et omni syrmate solutior qua caudae iacent, multicolor et discolor et versicolor, numquam ipsa, semper alia, etsi semper ipsa quando alia, totiens denique mutanda quotiens movenda.   [*On the Pallium*[16] 3.1–2]

---

14. In the year A.D. 68–69, following Nero's death, Galba, Otho, and Vitellius successively tried to retain control of the Roman state, and each died in the attempt. Vespasian's rule (69–79) restored some measure of stability to the imperial succession.

15. For a translation and further discussion of the letters, see C. R. Haines, *The Correspondence of Marcus Cornelius Fronto,* 2 vols., (London, 1919–1920); for the Latin text, see M. *Cornelii Frontonis Epistulae,* ed. M. P. J. van den Hout, vol. 1 (Leiden, 1954).

16. The *pallium* was a mantle worn by Greeks, especially philosophers; later in the same speech (5), Tertullian describes a decline in one's station in life as a movement "from the Roman toga to the pallium" (*a toga ad pallium*).

The verbal play of this passage is quite difficult to capture in translation. Eduard Norden regarded *On the Pallium* as the most difficult piece of writing in the Latin language.[17] The following version gives the sense of the passage but none of its glitter:

The beasts of the field also change their shape instead of their garment, and yet the peacock has plumage for its dress, indeed for its state dress; nay, richer by far on its neck bright with color than any hue of purple; more gilded in the gleaming of its back than any edging on a cloak; more unfettered where its tail does lie than any train on a robe; of many colors, varied colors, changing colors; never itself, always another, and yet always itself whenever another: in sum, mutable as often as it is movable.

The enthusiasms of Gellius, Fronto, and Tertullian point the way toward an order and a method for exploring the rhetorical artistry of *The Golden Ass*, beginning with its words—the building blocks, as it were, of second-century rhetoric—then following the developments of style through increasingly complex structures to the most ambitious edifices, descriptions of gods and prayers to them.

4

Every page of *The Golden Ass* is a mosaic that sparkles with glittering metaphors, archaisms, and newly coined words; with phrases that scan and rhyme like verse; with borrowings from the language of everyday proverbs, law, military science, religion, and medicine; with play on both the meaning and the sound of words. There is a fervor in these inventions that almost suggests desperation, as Apuleius first revives what an early stylist might have written, then tries to surpass it with an even more startling turn of phrase. To give only one example: Plautus had used *puellus* as the diminutive of *puer*; Cicero had employed *pulchellus* as a diminutive of the adjective *pulcher*; Apuleius tops both by stringing the two words together into one insinuating phrase, *tam venustum tamque pulchellum puellum*, "such a charm-

---

17. Norden, *Kunstprosa*, 615. On Tertullian as a Christian sophist, see T. D. Barnes, *Tertullian: An Historical and Literary Study* (Oxford, 1971), 211–232.

ing, pretty little laddie" (9.27). The example serves as an emblem of Apuleius' style. A good deal of the pleasure of his writing is to be found in its words. Most of the time it is not possible to reproduce their bizarre effect in a translation that aims to be faithful to the sense of the Latin.

The language of the novel constantly flatters its listeners, who are encouraged to delight in their superior knowledge and to listen to a flow of double meanings that no character in the novel is privileged to understand. Typical of ancient fiction, many of the characters have "eloquent" or "significant" names. When Psyche addresses her husband, Cupid, she speaks of the "soul of your sweet Psyche," *tuae Psychae dulcis anima* (5.6), a play on the Greek and Latin words for "soul" (*psychē, anima*). An innocent maiden is named Charite, suggesting the Greek *charis,* grace, charm (7.12). Her husband pretends to be a bloody robber and calls himself Haemus, a pun on Mount Haemus in Thrace, and also suggestive of *haima,* blood (7.5). A merchant is named Cerdo, after the Greek word for "gain" or "profit," *kerdos* (2.13). A wealthy man who gives animal shows to win the favor of his fellow citizens is called Demochares (4.13), suggesting the Greek *demos,* people, and *charis,* gratitude.

Apuleius also plays with the mere sound of words, as in the phrase *atra atria Proserpinae* (6.19), "the black entries of Proserpina"; Charite remains "unwilling in life," *invita . . . in vita* (8.6); a victim of fortune falls prey to an "unfavorable, I should rather say savage, luck," *fortunam scaevam an saevam verius dixerim miser incidit* (2.13). Very often the sounds of words complement their meaning. Thus Venus' gull is "a talkative bird, and rather curious," *haec illa verbosa et satis curiosa avis* (5.28); the ant who comes to Psyche's rescue appears in a string of appropriate diminutives, "that tiny little ant, little tiller of the field," *formicula illa parvula atque ruricola* (6.10); the reputation of Psyche's beauty "spreads abroad in a short time to the neighboring islands and many of the provinces of the earth," and does so in a fine alliterative style: "sic insulas iam *p*roximas et terrae *p*lusculum *p*rovinciasque *p*lurimas fama *p*orrecta *p*ervagatur" (4.29).

The *clausula* or rhythmical close of a period in a phrase or sentence is often composed in one or another poetic measure, such as the dactylic rhythms of

... mē pĕdĭ bús fŭgĭéntem ălĭénĭs
... fŏrmĭdánt ălĭí mĕlĭórĕm

The opening words of a sentence may just as likely have a metrical pattern, as in the measured words with which the household slave who reports the deaths of Tlepolemus and Charite begins his story:

oro, sŏllĭcítĭs ănĭmís ĭntĕndítĕ quórsŭm...

I ask you with sorrowful hearts to turn toward this tale of woe... [8.3]

Continually in the novel Apuleius' careful search for the right word leads to delight and surprise at an unexpected turn of phrase. The warning of the maid Fotis, for instance, is distinctly odd at first hearing:

quaecumque itaque commisero huius religiosi pectoris tui penetralibus, semper haec inter conseptum clausa custodias, oro, et simplicitatem relationis meae tenacitate taciturnitatis tuae remunerare.

Whatever I entrust then to the sanctuary of your religious breast I beg you to keep always closely concealed there. Reward by the strict seals of silence the honesty of my story.   [3.15]

To imitate the sound of Fotis' warning is risky business: a "simplicity of my relations held with the tenacity of your taciturnity." The effect is difficult to capture in English—at least in English that means anything. The passage recalls such early Roman poets as Plautus and their special addiction to alliteration; for example, a slave's words in the *Miles gloriosus* (404): "si ad erum haec res prius praevenit, peribis pulchre" ("If this news reaches our master first, you'll perish prettily"). Fotis speaks Latin *plautinissime*, in super-Plautine style.[18]

Even in a more formal setting the novel's language can be unpredictable. Here the opening of the speech by Haemus (actually Tlepolemus, the disguised husband of Charite) is pre-

18. The superlative is a coinage of Aulus Gellius (*Attic Nights* 3.4, 3.16).

sented in a way that shows the scheme of its rhymes, alliteration, and *clausulae:*

sic introgressus "havete" inquit	
"fortissimo deo Marti clientēs	11 syllables
mihique iam fidi commilitonēs	11 syllables
et *v*irum magnanimae *v*ivacitatis	
*v*olentēm *v*olentēs accipite	22 syllables (a *climax,* or rhetorical amplification, of 2 × 11 syllables)
libentius vulnera corpore excipientēm	
quam aurum manu suscipientēm	
ipsaque morte, quam formidant alii, meliorēm."	

Thus as he entered he said, "Hail, ye vassals of the stoutest warrior god Mars, now my trusty fellow campaigners, ye willing welcomers of a warrior of undaunted daring! Take me in, who suffer wounds on my body more freely than I take gold in my hand: a man who's better (and here's something others are afraid of) than death itself!" [7.5]

The eloquence of Haemus' bride, Charite, is of a different kind. As she stands over the unconscious form of the murderer and would-be adulterer Thrasyllus, her words suddenly turn into a coloratura aria about the hideous punishment in store for him. These murderous ideas are expressed through the trills and runs of

lumen certe nōn videbis,	8 syllables
manu comitis indigebis,	9 syllables
Chariten nōn tenebis,	7 syllables
nuptias nōn frueris,	7 syllables
nec mortis quiete recreaberis,	11 syllables
nec vitae voluptate laetaberis,	11 syllables

sed incertum simulacrum errabis inter Orcum et solem et diu quaeres dexteram, quae tuas expugnant pupulas quodque est in aerumna miserrimum, nescies de quo queraris.

It's certain you'll never more behold the light, you'll need a hand to lead you, you'll never hold Charite in your arms, you'll never enjoy a marriage, you'll neither rest in the peace of death nor rejoice in the pleasures of life, but you'll wander like a dim shadow between Orcus and the sun's light, and long you'll seek that hand which plucked out your eyes, and worst of all amid your misery, you'll never know whom you'll blame for this misfortune. [8.12]

Charite's speech—really an incantation—reveals an important aspect of the novel that might not be evident in translation. An apparently baffling prolixity is often caused by Apuleius' desire to enchant the ear of his listener. Here the rhymes and rhythms of Charite's tirade accentuate her vow to punish her husband's murderer.

Although stylistic variation abounds in Apuleius' work, his novel never attains the variety of characterizations so distinctive in Petronius' *Satyricon*. The qualities of Petronius' characters are reflected in their speech—from the extremes of Latinity and education of its intellectuals and poets to the vividly ignorant diction of the freedmen; all the common folk are as distinct from one another as they are from the polished and urbane narrator, Encolpius. At one point there is even an outburst against over-educated snobs (*Satyricon* 57–58). Such verisimilitude never appears in Apuleius. No matter how depraved a character may be, no matter how uncouth, his language is never anything less than elegant and grammatical. Even when a distraught Lucius is forced to defend himself against the charge of murder, he adjusts to the exigencies of the moment, remembers all his fine rhetorical training, and delivers a speech in an elegant periodic style that would have pleased Cicero himself:

I am not myself unmindful how hard it is, when the bodies of three citizens have been laid out in turn, for a man to defend himself against a murder charge; even when he speaks the truth and confesses to his every deed, it is nonetheless hard for him to persuade so great a multitude of his innocence. Still, if through your customary kindness you'll only bestow a hearing on me for a little while, I shall easily show you how it is that I wrongly bear a charge for a capital offense that came about, not through my doing, but by a fortuitous turn of events that was marked by a perfectly understandable anger on my part. [3.4]

This passage is a classic example of an *exordium*, or opening section of an oration. It is designed to soothe the apprehensions of the listeners, gain their attention, and flatter their egos by an excessively modest portrait of the speaker's abilities. Classical oratory abounds with examples; Cicero's *For Milo* begins *etsi vereor* . . ., "Though I am apprehensive. . . ." and then proceeds in a fashion that is anything but apprehensive. A particularly notable feature of Lucius' forensic style is his fondness for the *clausula* ‒‒‒. It appears five times in the first two sentences and is accentuated by the rhyme of the two infinitives *persuadere* and *sustinere*.

> nec ipse ignoro, quam sit arduum
>> trinis civium corporibus expositis
>> eum qui caedis arguatur
>> quamvis vera dicat
>> et de facto confiteatur ultro
>> tamen tantae multitudini
>> quod sit innocens persuadere.
> sed si paulisper audientiam publica mihi tribuerit
>> humanitas
>> facile vos edocebo
>>> me discrimen capitis non meo merito
>>> sed rationabilis indignationis eventu fortuitu
>> tantam criminis invidiam frustra sustinere.

To have rhyming *clausulae* was considered unacceptable before Apuleius' day. Quintilian had expressly advised against the combination, which he felt imparted a puerile tone to one's prose style (10.2.21).

Descriptive passages can be enlivened by rhymes or elaborate parallel constructions. At the opening of Book 1, Lucius' crossing the mountains of Thessaly is portrayed in a monotonous clippity-clop of dactyls, with rhymes of *o* that turn the horse's rubdown into a little jingle:

> postquam ardua montium
>> et lubrica vallium
>> et roscida cespitum
>> et glebosa camporum emersimus
> equo indigena peralbo vehens iam eo quoque admodum fesso,
> ut ipse etiam fatigationem sedentariam incessus discuterem,

in pedes desilio
equi sudorem fronte curiose exfrico
auris remulceo
frenos detraho
in gradum lenem sensim proveho
quoad lassitudinis incommodum alvi solitum ac naturale
praesidium eliquare.

After we traversed the tops of mountains and the sides of valleys, the
dews of the grass and the furrowed fields, borne along on a white
horse, which was a thoroughbred from that region, I noticed he was
also rather tired from the journey; to shake off the weariness from
sitting so long, I leaped to the ground. I carefully wiped the sweat from
the horse's brow, I stroked his ears, I loosened his bridle, I led him
forward at a gradual pace to allow him to restore himself with the
customary food that nature would supply. [1.2]

An evil wife is described by a series of rhyming adjectives:

nec enim vel unum vitium nequissimae illi feminae deerat, sed
omnia prorsus ut in quandam caenosam latrinam in eius animum
flagitia confluxerant:
saeva
scaeva
virosa
ebriosa
pervicax
pertinax
in rapinis turpibus avara
in sumptibus foedis profusa
inimica fidei
hostis pudicitiae.

There was not a single vice lacking in this vilest of women; all kinds of
sin had flowed into her spirit as though into some filthy cesspool. She
was savage and crude, poisonous and drunken, overbearing and in-
domitable; grasping in base thefts, extravagant in debased living, an
enemy of fidelity, a foe of chastity. [9.14]

In both these passages, rhyme accentuates the parallel phrasing.

The six syllables of *ardua montium* are echoed three times:

ārdŭă mōntĭŭm
lūbrĭcă vāllĭŭm
rōscĭdă cēspĭtŭm
glēbōsă cāmpōrŭm (breaks rhythm by substituting two - and one ˘ for one - and two ˘; i.e., - ˘ ˘ → - - ˘).

Similarly, a jingle arises in the second passage by a change of one or more letters within the initial word:

saeva → *sc*aeva
virosa → *ebri*osa
pervicax → per*tin*ax

The most elaborate style is reserved for descriptions of or addresses to divinities, as in the description of Cupid asleep on his couch after Psyche's discovery of her mysterious husband. The scene inspires an *ecphrasis* of a favorite motif in Hellenistic art. Apuleius surrounds the phrase *ipsum illum Cupidinem* ("that very Cupid himself") with many syllables containing the same liquid and nasal consonants (*l, r, m, n*) and vowels (*i, u*):

sed *cum primum lum*inis ob*l*atione to*ri* sec*re*ta *claru*erunt, videt *omnium* fe*rarum mitissimam dulcissimam*que besti*am, ipsum illum Cupidinem formonsum* de*um formon*se *cubantem,* cuius aspect*u lucer*nae quoque *lumen* hi*laratum* in*crebru*it et a*cum*inis sac*rile*gi novac*ula* praenitebat.

But as soon as the lamp was raised on high, the mysteries of her bed shone forth: she saw the gentlest and sweetest of all wild creatures, that very Cupid himself, a beautiful god beautifully lying. At his appearance the cheerful flame burned higher and the dagger repented its sacrilegious edge. [5.22]

The sound of *ipsum illum Cupidinem* spreads mellifluously throughout the sentence. Apuleius then goes on to describe the appearance of the sleeping god, striving now not so much for aural effects as for vivid images. The key to that vividness lies in the adjectives of the sentence:

videt capitis *aurei genialem* caesariem *ambrosia temulentam,* cervices *lacteas* genasque *purpureas pererrantes* crinium globos *decoriter impeditos,*

20. Cupid and Psyche on an Oxyrhynchus papyrus. Reproduced from Kurt Weitzmann, *Ancient Book Illumination*, Martin Classical Lectures 16 (Cambridge, Mass., 1959), Fig. 117, Plate 57, by permission of the Trustees of Oberlin College and the Museo Archeologico, Florence.

alios *antependulos*, alios *retropendulos*, quorum splendore *nimio ful-gurante* iam et ipsum lumen lucernae vacillabat; per umeros *volatilis* dei pinnae *roscidae micanti* flore candicant et quamvis alis quiescentibus *extimae* plumulae *tenellae* ac *delicatae tremule resultantes inquieta* las-civiunt: ceterum corpus *glabellum* atque *luculentum* et *quale* peperisse Venerem non paeniteret. Ante lectuli pedes iacebat arcus et pharetra et sagittae, *magni* dei *propitia* tela.

She saw the delightful hair on his golden head dripping with ambrosia, the flowing curls of his locks gracefully entangled over his milk-white breast and ruddy cheeks, some hanging down in front, and some hang-ing down behind; the flame of the lamp itself fluttered at this over-whelming splendor. On the shoulders of the winged god there bloomed dewy plumes of sparkling whiteness, and although the wings themselves were at rest, the fine down on the end of delicate feathers rippled tremblingly in restless movement. The rest of his body was smooth and luscious; to such a one Venus would not have regretted giving birth. Before the legs of his couch lay bow, quiver, and arrows, gracious weapons of the great god. [5.22]

The *ecphrasis* is an attempt to challenge the visual arts and possibly surpass them. Aided by words, the mind's eye may construct a vision surpassing anything achieved by the painter or the sculptor.

Last, we come to the long prayers and speeches of Book 11. Here Apuleius is at his most ambitious. After the book has opened with Lucius' prayer to the Queen of Heaven (11.2), Isis begins her reply in this way:

Behold, Lucius, I am moved by your prayers: I, the mother of the nature of things, the mistress of all the elements, the first offspring of the ages, the supreme divinity, the queen of the spirits of the dead, the first among those in heaven, the uniform manifestation of gods and goddesses, who govern by my will the crests of light in the sky, the purifying streams of ocean, and the lamented silence of those below; whose one and only godhead is venerated all over the earth under many forms, with varying rites, with manifold name. Thence the firstborn Phrygians call me Pessinuntia, mother of the gods; the aborig-inal people of Attica call me Cecropian Minerva; the Cyprians moving over the waves call me Venus of Paphos; the archer Cretans call me Diana of Mount Dictys; the three-tongued Sicilians call me Stygian Proserpina; the Eleusinians call me the ancient goddess Ceres; some call me Juno, others Bellona; some Hecate, others Rhamnusia; but those who are enlightened by the beginning rays of the rising sun, the Ethiopians, the Africans, and those who excel in ancient lore, the Egyptians, all these worship me with proper ceremonies and call me by my true name, Queen Isis. [11.5]

This is an aretalogy, or praise of a god's virtues (*aretai*). Like the hymns of Isidorus, which date from the Hellenistic period, this speech emphasizes Isis' supreme powers.[19] An interesting parallel from Apuleius' own times, in no way artistically comparable to the hymns of Isidorus, can be seen in the Isis aretalogy from Cyme in the Aeolid, set up sometime in the second century A.D. by Demetrius, son of Artemidorus:

I am Isis, the ruler of every land, instructed by Hermes, the one who learned from him both the sacred and the profane letters, so that all things might not be written the same way.

I set the laws for men, and set them in such a way that no one could change them.

I am the eldest daughter of Kronos.

I am the wife and sister of Osiris the king.

I am the finder of fruit for men.

I am the mother of Horos the king.

I am the one ordained in the star of the Dog.

I am the god called on by women.

I am the founder of the city Boubastos.

I separated earth from heaven.

I marked out the paths for the stars.

I made a way of passage for the sun and the moon.

I founded the toils of the sea.

I made justice firm and secure.

I brought together man and woman.

So the list runs, through fifty-six powers, ending with

19. The four hymns of Isidorus were composed in verse and incised in stone; see Vera F. Vanderlip, *The Four Greek Hymns of Isidorus and the Cult of Isis* (Toronto, 1972), and her translation of Hymn 1 in Appendix 3.

I conquer what was destined.
Listen to what is decreed.
Hail to thee, Egypt, thou who nourished me.[20]

This is not a work of art, but for the devotee, who already knows Isis' power and the truth of her religion, the list is sufficient in itself and requires no elaboration. The Cyme aretalogy records a series of self-evident facts about the divinity, rather like the doctrines embodied within a Christian catechism.

The "self-predication" of Isis in Apuleius' work is much more ambitious. While the Cyme aretalogy is in itself no mean feat of devotion, Apuleius arranges Isis' powers in an artistically compelling way that makes the prose version seem quite plain. Schematic arrangement of the original reveals astonishing care for structure, rhythm, and rhyme. Apuleius produced a piece of prose even more complicated than the hexameters of Isidorus:

I. En adsum tuis commota, Luci, precibus,

A.	re*rum*	naturae	parens,
	elemento*rum*	omnium	domina,
	saeculo*rum*	progenies	initialis,
B.		summ*a* numin*um*	
		regin*a* mani*um*	
		prim*a* caelit*um*,	

deorum   dearumque   facie   uniformis,

C.	quae	caeli	luminos*a*	culmin*a*,
		maris	salubri*a*	flamin*a*,
		infernum	deplorat*a*	silenti*a*,

nutibus meis dispenso:

D.	cuius	numen	unicum
		*multi*formi	speci*e*,
		ritu	vario,
		nomin*e*	*multi*iugo

20. Werner Peek, *Der Isishymnus von Andros und verwandte Texte* (Berlin, 1930), 122–124.

totus venerator orbis.

II. A.

inde	primigenii	Phryges	Pessinuntiam	deum matrem,
hinc	autochthones	Attici	Cecropeiam	Minervam,
illinc	fluctuantes	Cyprii	Paphiam	Venerem,

B.

	Cretes	Sagittiferi	Dictynnam	Dianam,
	Siculi	trilingues	Stygiam	Proserpinam,
	Eleusinii	vetustam	deam	Cererem,

C.

		Iunonem	alii,
		Bellonam	alii,
		Hecatam	isti,
		Rhamnusiam	ilii,

D. et qui nascentis dei Solis
inchoantibus illustrantur radiis
Aethiopes Ariique
priscaque doctrina pollentes
Aegyptii caeremoniis me propriis percolentes
appellant vero nomine
Reginam Isidem.[21]

A detailed analysis of this passage might mention such subtleties as the way the revelation of Isis is cast into two long
sentences, each with its elements carefully arranged. For example, in sentence I, the groups of words in sections A–D are
arranged in a strophe–antistrophe pattern, so that section A has
groups of three words; section C, also groups of three; and
sections B and D, groups of two words each. Sentence II unfolds
in different but equally schematic patterns, with section A having five words in each phrase, section B four, and section C two.
Section D breaks the patterns of symmetry with its long relative
qui clause ("those who . . ."). The sentence concludes with the
naming of Isis' most important worshipers, the Egyptians, and
finally, the name of Isis herself. Frequently rhyme marks off
each period, so that a listener could easily hear the different

21. This scheme is adapted from Bernhard, *Der Stil des Apuleius*, 23–26; for
Apuleius' fondness for triads and other numerical patterns, see ibid., 116–119.

groups. To summarize the architecture of the two sentences, here is a more skeletal outline:

I.   A. 1 (three words)   C. 1 (three words)
               2   2
               3   3

     B. 1 (two words)   D. 1 (two words)
               2   2
               3   3

II.   A. 1 (five words)
               2
               3

     B. 1 (four words)
               2
               3

     C. 1 (two words)
                2
               3

     D. Asymetrical group

Within each group of Part II, careful attention is given to the order of the syntactic units, so that the sequence of epithet–subject–object in IIA is reversed to subject–epithet–object in IIB:

| primigenii | Phryges | Pessinuntiam deum matrem |
| Cretes | sagittiferi | Dictynnam Dianam |

the firstborn Phrygians, Pessinuntia, mother of the gods
the arrow-bearing Cretans, Diana of Mount Dictys

To trace every aspect of Apuleius' preoccupation with this sort of calculation would lead us toward a subject rather different from the basic concern of this chapter, the language of the novel. For he was interested not only in the choice of words and their arrangement in a sentence but in their total number as well. Lucius' speech to the Queen of Heaven contains some 166 words, which happens to be the sum of words in Psyche's two prayers to Ceres and Juno in Book 6 (cf. 6.2, 6.4, and 11.2). Presumably Isis' supremacy over all other goddesses is reflected in the number of words required to pray to her. Whether this kind of subtlety could possibly be caught during a recital of the novel is debatable. When we reach the point where we are not so much listening to language as counting words on a page, more than one reader may be tempted to conclude that Apuleius has entered the company of the Joyce of *Finnegans Wake*. Yet the kind of calculations outlined here, if on the level of grade school arithmetic, are evidently of some theological as well as literary significance.

CHAPTER 6

The Reader as Listener

They say that nature gave each of us two ears and one tongue
because we ought to talk less and listen more.
— Plutarch, *How to Listen to Lectures* 39B

Any good sophist required an appreciative audience, and I
hope readers of this book will now be disposed to extend that
courtesy to Apuleius and *The Golden Ass*. Apuleius was clearly
scrupulous about the kind of writing that mattered most to him.
It is writing in which even today's reader may still find much
pleasure. He arranged the novel in eleven books, not
haphazardly but with obvious care; he did not find the combination of the ten books of Lucius' adventures with the eleventh Isis
book a problem, but rather a great opportunity to display his
literary and philosophical talents to their fullest; and the language of every part of the novel is, by standards of Apuleius'
day, elegant and pleasing to the ear. The novel reveals on every
page its author's design for recitation.

As with the controversy between analysts and unitarians in
Homeric scholarship, it is fruitful to compare these features of
The Golden Ass with the compositional techniques that gave the
Iliad and the *Odyssey* their distinctive form. With Apuleius, as
with Homer, we must realize that a reading of their works that
ignores the circumstances of their composition will be not only
unfair but, from a historical and esthetic point of view, anachro-
nistic. That is to say, Homeric verse was not composed in writing for a literate society, but rather orally, for delivery to an
audience. And Apuleius' novel, like almost everything else he
left us, was in the first instance designed to be heard by an
audience as well. As Wagner's *Die Meistersinger* shows, there is

a place for Beckmesser in the world of art, but sooner or later Walther von Stolzing must be allowed to sing his prize song.

It follows that *The Golden Ass* should, if at all possible, be recited; ideally it should be recited in Apuleius' Latin. No translation in any modern language comes close to the inimitable sounds of the original. Some future version may reproduce more fully the aural qualities of the novel; it would be a task roughly on the order of translating James Joyce into another language. Yet the enterprise would be well worth the effort. The language of *The Golden Ass* contains as many surprises for an audience of listeners as its strange and unexpected twists of plot provide for a reader.

An anecdote in Philostratus about Favorinus, a fellow sophist of Apuleius (fl. A.D. 150), suggests that it would be difficult to overestimate the centrality of the sheer sound of words to one's literary experience in the second century: "When he delivered discourses at Rome, everyone was interested in them, even those who did not understand a word of Greek at all; for he enchanted them by the tone of his voice and by the expression of his face and by the rhythm of his speech" (*Lives of the Sophists* 491). Here was the essence of the sophist's art. Apuleius' tone of voice, facial expression, and rhythm of speech must have added dimensions to the experience of listening to his novel that we can now only dimly imagine. Such was the art of the novel as Apuleius conceived it for *The Golden Ass,* as different in its way from the one Henry James was later to describe as could be imagined. Lucius' odyssey toward Queen Isis was as much a virtuoso exercise as anything else Apuleius ever wrote.

APPENDIX 1

Five Selections from Apuleius' Florida

The Golden Ass is sometimes taken to be a notable departure from Apuleius' other writings. This opinion might possibly be substantiated by those of his works that are now lost. But on the basis of the writings that have survived, such a view has little to recommend it. The novel is far from being the frivolous scribbling of an otherwise austere Platonist. Of course, the fiction of any period will likely be regarded as less serious than philosophical or religious writing. As far as this book is concerned, that possibility will remain an interesting and unexplored problem of literary criticism.

The purple patches from the *Florida* are entirely typical of the literary tastes of Apuleius' day. There is no translation of more recent date than H. E. Butler's, and his version is not widely available.[1] Three examples from the collection (5, 14, and 20) have already been quoted, in Chapter 4.

The first two selections presented here (12 and 19) appeal to an audience's love for the bizarre and the miraculous—two themes announced in the opening chapter of *The Golden Ass*. Number 13 is yet another indication that philosophy and oratory were identical occupations for Apuleius. The last two selections (9 and 16) illustrate the virtuoso quality of Apuleius' performance as a sophist. Whether in a theater at Carthage or through the *persona* of the narrator of his novel, Apuleius never fails to draw the audience's attention to himself.

A useful introduction to the literary theories and practices that

1. *The Apology and Florida of Apuleius of Madaura,* trans. H. E. Butler (Oxford, 1909).

typify the *Florida* can be found in S. F. Bonner, *Roman Declamation* (Liverpool, 1949); Dorothy M. Brock, *Studies in Fronto and His Age* (Cambridge, 1911); and Michael Winterbottom, ed. and trans., *Seneca the Elder: Declamations*, 2 vols., Loeb Classical Library (London and Cambridge, Mass., 1974). The only full-length study on the *Florida* is Fabian Opeku's dissertation, "A Commentary with Introduction on the *Florida* of Apuleius" (London, 1974).

12: The Parrot[2]

The parrot is a bird that is a bird of India. In size it is only a very little less large than the dove, but its color is not that of a dove: for it is not milky white or dull blue, either blended or distinct, or pinkish or speckled. No, the color of the parrot is green, both in its inner plumage and its outer broomage,[3] except that its neck alone is different from all the rest. For its little neck is encircled and crowned by a little red band, like a golden necklace and of equal splendor. Its beak is extremely tough. When in its flight it hurtles down in an enormous sweep on some rock, it fixes itself there with its beak as though with an anchor. Its head also is as tough as its beak. When it is compelled to imitate our speech, its head is struck with a little iron key, so that it comes to understand the command of its master. This is the schoolmaster's rod by which it learns its lesson. It learns right away so long as it is a chick, up to the age of two years, so long as its mouth can be molded and its tongue is supple enough to be put into movement. But if it is captured when it is old, it is both unteachable and forgetful.

Now a parrot is more disposed to learn human speech if it feeds on nuts and if it has five toes on its feet, like a man. Not all parrots have that distinguishing mark, but it is a common prop-

2. This kind of *tour de force* was popular with sophists in Apuleius' day. Dio Chrysostom wrote a *Eulogy of the Gnat* and a *Praise of the Parrot*, and Fronto composed a *Praise of Smoke* and a *Praise of Dust*.

3. The Latin is a typical jingle: *et intimis plumulis et extimis palmulis*.

erty to all of them to have a tongue broader than the tongues of other birds. By this means they articulate human speech more easily because of their wider plectrum and palate. But it sings to us what it learns—or rather it speaks it, so that you would think it was a man. Listen, though, to the crow as it tries to talk: it only crows, it doesn't talk at all. But for all that, both the crow and the parrot say nothing else but what they have learned to speak. If you teach the parrot curses, it will curse all day and all night long, screaming all the time with oaths. This is its song, this it considers a melody. When it has run through all the curses it has learned, it starts the same song all over again. If you want to be rid of its cursing, its tongue has to be cut out, or the bird must be sent back as soon as possible into its woods.

19: *Asclepiades and the Dead Man*

The famous Asclepiades,[4] among the princes of medicine—if you make the exception of Hippocrates, the greatest of them all—was the first to discover the uses of wine as a remedy for sick people, with the proviso, of course, that it be given at the right time. He was extremely clever in detecting that very point, as he had made a most careful study of abnormal and rapid pulse in the arteries. One day when he was returning by chance to the city from his farmhouse in the nearby countryside, he beheld on the outskirts of the town a large funeral ceremony, which a vast number of people were attending in a throng. They were standing around in the very depths of grief, all dressed in worn and ragged garments. Since no one replied to his questions, he drew nearer out of a natural curiosity to learn the identity of the dead man—or perhaps to observe so that he might add something to his profession. There is no question that he changed the fate of the man lying there, very nearly buried in the earth.

All parts of the poor wretch's body were already suffused

4. He lived in the first century B.C.

with perfumes, his face already smeared with odorous oint-
ments; the preparation of the body was finished, it was ready to
be carried to the funeral pyre. Asclepiades observed certain
signs very closely, tapped the body again and again, and discovered that life was still concealed within it. At once he cried
out, "The man is alive! Take away the torches! Put out the fire!
Pull down the funeral pyre! Carry the funeral banquet from the
tomb back to the dining table!" Thereupon a murmur arose.
Some people thought that the doctor ought to be believed, others went so far as to make fun of doctoring in general. Eventually, even though the man's relatives were unwilling (either because now they would get no inheritance or because they still
did not believe the doctor), Asclepiades at last just barely obtained a brief delay for the dead man and brought him back to
the door of his house. The man was snatched from the hands of
the undertakers—as it were from the jaws of Hades itself.
Straightaway he restored the breath of life; straightaway with
certain medicines he called forth the soul that was lurking in the
invisible recesses of the body.[5]

13. The Eloquence of a Philosopher is Compared to the Song of Certain Birds

... For philosophy has not bestowed on me speech of the
kind that nature supplies to certain birds, a brief song suited for
a certain hour: a morning song for swallows, a midday song for
cicadas,[6] a late song for night owls, an afternoon song for buzzards, an evening song for screech owls, a night song for horned
owls, a predawn song for roosters. All of these creatures differ
both in the times at which they begin to sing their songs and in
the way they sing them. The roosters sing with a reveille call,
the horned owls with a little moan, the screech owls with a

5. The theme of this selection appears also in *The Golden Ass:* cf. Thelyphron's
tale in Book 2 and the tale of the wise doctor in Book 10.
6. The song of the cicada evidently qualifies this insect for inclusion among
what are otherwise its natural predators.

complaint, the buzzards with a distorted sound, the cicadas with a strident rasp, the swallows with a shrill call. But with philosophy, both its reasoning and its eloquence are appropriate for every time of day. In hearing it is worthy of respect, in understanding it is profitable, and in music it sounds all the tunes.

9: A Discourse in the Theater at Carthage, in Which Apuleius Commends His Audience's Taste, Compares His Talents with Those of the Sophist Hippias, and Praises the Departing Proconsul Severianus[7]

If by chance anyone sitting in this fine assembly is one of my envious detractors—since in a great city this kind of person is also found, who prefers to belittle his betters rather than to imitate them; who affects to hate those whom he has no hope of equaling; one who, since his own name is obscure, would become known by using mine—if, I say, any of those jealous people has forced himself like some blemish upon this most brilliant audience, I should like him for just a little while to run his eyes over this amazing assembly, and, having considered how large this crowd is (such as before my time was never seen gathered to hear a philosopher), let him consider in his own mind how much danger there is to the reputation of a man who has not been accustomed to be despised; for it is an arduous and extremely difficult task to satisfy even the moderate expectations of a few people, especially for me: the reputation I have acquired and your favorable disposition toward me would not allow me to utter anything carelessly and without deep thought.

For who of you would forgive me a single mistake in grammar? Who would acquit me of one syllable's mispronunciation? Who would permit me rashly to blabber out rude and corrupt words as they occurred, like a madman? These are things you easily pardon in others—and rightly so—but you scrutinize closely every single thing I say; you weigh it out with

---

7. Severianus' tenure in office enables us to date this piece to A.D. 162–164.

a fine measure; you test it with a file and rule; you check its smoothness by the lathe and its seriousness by the buskin of tragedy. Modest accomplishment meets with as much excuse as genuine merit meets with difficulty. So do I acknowledge my difficulty: I ask nothing but that you apply the same standard to me as before.

Nor should you let a small and spurious likeness mislead you; for as I have often said, strolling beggary walks about cloaked in the robe of philosophy. The public crier in the proconsul's service ascends the tribunal and is seen wearing the toga there; indeed, he stands there a long time or walks about or cries out with all his might at the top of his voice; but the proconsul himself discourses in a moderate tone, infrequently, while seated, and often reads from a tablet. For the crier, incessant speech is the function of his office; but the proconsul's tablet yields a sentence that, once it has been recited, can neither be increased nor diminished by so much as one letter. No, as soon as the sentence has been read, it is put into the archives of the province.

I myself also suffer something like this in the course of my own profession. For whatever I offer to you is taken up at once and read, nor can I call it back to change or emend anything therein. Thus I must be all the more scrupulous in my speech, and indeed not only in one kind of study. For more works of mine are in existence in the realm of the Muses than of Hippias in his handicrafts.[8] What does that mean? Pay close attention and I will explain in exact detail.

Hippias was one of the number of sophists. By the abundance of his talents he was superior to everyone, in eloquence second to none. He lived at the same time Socrates did; his homeland was Elis. His family was unknown, but his fame was vast, his fortune small, his genius illustrious, his memory excellent, his studies varied, his rivals many. This Hippias once came to Pisa when the Olympic games were being held, where he was no less deserving of admiration for the ornaments he wore than for the

---

8. Hippias lived ca. 485–415 B.C. Plato's dialogues *Hippias Major* and *Hippias Minor* reveal that the eulogy that follows—which mentions only Hippias' handicrafts—is rather one-sided.

fact that he had made them. For all that he had with him he had made with his very own hands and had not purchased a single thing: the garments with which he was clad and the sandals with which he was shod and the jewels with which he was conspicuous. For clothing he had as undergarment a tunic that was of fine thread, triple woven, and dyed twice with purple; he had woven this at home, all by himself. He had a belt decorated with Babylonian decoration of wonderful colors. No one had helped him with this, either. He had a cloak of white which he wore as an outer garment; that cloak is known also to have come from his own labors. And likewise he had fashioned the sandals that covered his feet; and likewise the gold ring he wore on his left hand, which had a most artistically made signet. He had closed the circle of the ring and sealed the bezel and engraved the gem.

I have not yet told you all he did! Why should I regret mentioning what he himself was not ashamed to display? He asserted in a large assembly that he himself had also made an oil flask that he carried around with him. It was shaped like a flat sphere, round in its line, and compressed in shape. Along with it he had an elegant little strigil, with a straight little handle and a hollow tongue to the spoon, so that one might hold it easily in the hand and the sweat might flow out of it in a stream.

Who will not praise a man so skilled in so many arts, so illustrious for such comprehensive knowledge, so skilled a Daedalus in the use of so many tools? To be sure, I praise Hippias, but I prefer to rival his richness in matters of learning rather than in matters of personal appurtenances. For I confess indeed that I am of little skill in the manual arts. I buy my garments from a clothier, these shoes from the shoemaker. I do not wear a ring, but regard gems and gold as worth nothing more than lead and pebbles. I purchase my strigil and oil flask and other utensils for the bath at the market. No, I will not deny it, I do not know how to use the loom or the awl or the file or the lathe or any other implements of that kind, but in their place I much prefer to compose with a single pen poems of all kinds appropriate to the laurel branch, the lyre, the comic sock, the tragic buskin; likewise satires and riddles; likewise various kinds of histories and some orations praised by the discerning and some dialogues praised by the philosophers. I do all of these things and others like them as much in Greek as in Latin, with a twofold desire, equal zeal, and similar style.

Would that I were able to heap up all these things before you, O excellent proconsul, not one by one and separately, but all together and in a heap, and then enjoy your renowned testimony for all our labors with the Muses! It is not, indeed, because of lack of fame (which has long been maintained for me unbroken and flourishing by all of your predecessors down to you yourself), but because I want no one to have more esteem for me than that man whom I rightly esteem above all others.[9] For it is a law of nature that him whom you praise, him also you love; and further, that him whom you love, by him also do you want to be praised. And I confess that I am one who cherishes you, though I am bound to you by no private but rather by every kind of public favor. I have indeed obtained nothing from you, because I asked for nothing. But philosophy has taught me to love not only an act of kindness, but also an act of unkindness; to listen rather to the voice of justice than to serve my own interests; to prefer what is in the common interest to what is in my own. Therefore, while many others take delight in the actual fruits of your goodness, I delight simply in the zeal with which your goodness is inspired.

I began that practice at the time I considered your governance of the affairs of the citizens of this province. For what you did, those who have experienced your kindness ought to love you the more intensely, and even those who have not should do so because of your example. For you have benefited many by your kindness and have rendered everyone a service by your example. Who would not love to learn from you the moderation by which they might obtain your pleasant seriousness, mild austerity, calm firmness, and charming vigor?

To my knowledge Africa has had no proconsul whom she

9. Flattery of high officials was a stock in trade of rhetoricians during the Empire. The best-known speech of this kind, far more effusive than even this sample, is Pliny the Younger's *Panegyricus* (delivered ca. A.D. 100). In it Pliny praises Trajan and draws unfavorable comparisons between him and his predecessor, Domitian (died A.D. 96).

revered more or feared less. In no other year of office but yours has shame rather than fear proved enough to check crime. No other person with your power has more often helped and more rarely terrified. No one has ever raised a son more like his father in virtue than yours. And thus none of our pronconsuls has resided in Carthage longer than you have. When you made a tour of the province and Honorinus stayed with us, we felt your absence less, although we longed all the more for your return. In the son there is the fairness of the father, in the young man the prudence of an old one, in the deputy is the authority of the consul. So truly does he offer up an image of all your good qualities that—and I call Heaven to witness—there would be more praise for the son than for you, were it not that you had imparted it to him! Would that we might enjoy his company always! What mean these changes of proconsuls to us, what these brief years and rapidly passing months? Oh, how swiftly pass the days when good men are with us! Oh, how hurried the tenure in office of the best governors! Now, Severianus, our entire province grieves at your departure! But even so, Honorinus is called by his own merits to the praetorship; and the favor of the two Caesars[10] prepares him for the consulate; today our affection lays claim on him. And we in Carthage find hope for the future only in the consolation of your example; he who is dispatched now as deputy will return swiftly to us as proconsul.

16: A Speech of Thanks to the Magistrate Aemilianus Strabo and the People and Senate of Carthage for Erecting a Statue of Apuleius; in Which is Told the Story of the Death of the Comic Poet Philemon[11]

Before beginning, illustrious citizens of Africa, to thank you for the statue you kindly proposed when I was present and did

10. Marcus Aurelius and Lucius Verus.
11. Apuleius here expounds the well-worn theme of the comedy of life versus the comedy of the stage ("O Menander and life, which one of you imitated the other?"). As noted in Chapter 2, the Festival of Laughter in Book 3 of *The Golden Ass* plays with the same idea.

me the honor of decreeing when I was away, I first want to explain to you why I have been for a number of days away from this theater, and why I took myself off to the Persian Waters (a most pleasing place to swim for those who have their health, and a curative one to those who are sick). For I have resolved that I shall render an account to you of all my time: you to whom I have resolutely dedicated myself for all time to come. Never will I do anything so important or so trivial but that you will both know about it and be the judge of it.

Why then did I take myself away so suddenly from the sight of your most illustrious company? I shall relate to you a practically exact parallel about how suddenly unforeseen dangers befall men by telling you of the comic poet Philemon. You are well enough informed about his talent; now learn a little about his death. Or would you also like me to say something about his talent?

This Philemon was a poet, a writer of middle comedy, a producer of plays for the stage during the time of Menander, with whom he competed.[12] Not equal to him, perhaps, but his rival all the same; indeed, he defeated Menander in contests more times than it is decent to talk about. Still, you can find a great deal of wit in him: plots charmingly entangled; recognitions clearly made out; characters set in the proper situations; aphorisms true to life; funny things (but not unworthy of what comedy should be); serious things (but not so serious as genuine tragedy would be). In his works seductions are rare, mistakes perfectly safe to make, love affairs acknowledged. All the same in him you will still find the lying pimp and the passionate lover and the clever slave and the coquettish mistress and the shrewish wife and the indulgent mother and the scolding uncle and the helpful comrade and the fighting soldier, and yes, gnawing parasites and stingy parents and wanton courtesans.

These qualities had for a long time made him famous in the art of comedy. One day he was by chance reciting part of a play he had recently written. He was in the middle of the third act and was stirring up those rather pleasant feelings (which is the sort

12. Philemon (ca. 368–267 B.C.) was actually a poet of the new comedy.

of thing that comedy loves to have happen) when suddenly there came a shower of rain—as just recently happened to me—which compelled him to dismiss the throng in the auditorium and postpone the treat for his audience. But since a great many people asked him to finish, he was prepared to read the rest of the play the very next day.

Accordingly on the following day a vast crowd of people eagerly assembled. Everyone sat as close to the front as he could; the latecomer nodded to the friends who had reserved a seat for him; every person who was squeezed out of his place in the front rows complained; then when the whole theater was crammed full with the mob, a buzz of conversation began to rise. Those who had not been present to hear what had been read thus far began to ask questions about what they had missed; those who had been there began to tell what they knew. When everyone knew what had been said, they awaited what was to follow.

Meanwhile the day passed on by, and Philemon did not come to the assembly. Some people grumbled at the tardiness of the poet, many defended him. But when the delay was longer than anyone could reasonably expect and Philemon still did not appear, some of the readier members of the audience were sent to fetch him—and found him dead in his very own bed. He had just given up the ghost and was growing stiff in death; he lay there reclining on his couch as though thinking. His hand was still holding the scroll, his face was still directed down to the book, but now it was empty of all signs of life: he was oblivious of his book and regardless of his audience. Those who had come in stood around for a little while, stunned at such an unexpected situation, at the marvel of such a fine death. Then they returned to the theater and told the audience that the poet Philemon, who had been expected to finish a fictional plot in the theater, had finished the real drama at home. For he had said to human affairs, "Farewell" and "Give me your applause";[13] but to his friends "Grieve" and "Give me your tears." "Yesterday's

---

13. The traditional close to a Roman comedy was "Farewell" (*valete*) and "Give us your applause" (*plaudite*).

shower was an augury of our tears of today," they said; "his comedy finished with the funeral torch rather than with the torch of a comedy's bridal procession. Since this excellent poet has made an exit from his role in life, it is fitting that we now exit from the auditorium to his funeral. First his bones must be collected; after that, the poems."

I learned a long time ago that these events happened the way I have recalled them, but I brought them to mind again today, mindful of my own peril. For as you will recall, when my recitation was interrupted by a rainstorm, I postponed it to the following day at your request, indeed very much as in the manner of Philemon. And on that very same day I sprained my ankle in the exercise hall so violently that I very nearly tore the joint from the leg; it was only dislocated, however, and is still swollen from that dislocation.[14] I put it back into place with a great force, and for quite a while was rigid with rivers of sweat. Then a vicious pain began to spread throughout my bowels and was brought under control only a little while before it had practically finished me off and forced me in the manner of Philemon to be rather dead than read, to finish first what was fated for *me* before finishing what I was fated to say, to polish off my life instead of my discourse.[15] As soon therefore as I had recovered the power to walk at the Persian Waters (I was aided as much by their mild temperature as by their soothing application—not, indeed, so much as to be able to race to you, but enough to be able to hurry to you), I came to deliver what was promised. In the meantime, by your kindness you have not only taken away my lameness but also added fleetness to my feet.

Yet why should I not hasten back to pronounce profuse thanks to you for an honor for which I myself never asked? It is true that the grandeur of Carthage is so great that a philosopher

14. Everything about a sophist could be interesting, even his upper and lower intestinal tracts; for an entire work devoted to confessions of bodily ailments, see Aristides' *Sacred Tales*.

15. The original is a series of puns that are difficult to reproduce in a literal translation: *ante letum abire quam lectum* ("to go off to my grave rather than to my reading"), *potius implere fata quam fanda* ("to finish my destiny rather than my speech"), *consummare potius animam quam historiam* ("to bring my life rather than my account to its close").

would be honored to beg from her; yet still your kindness should be whole and inviolate. No personal request of mine should detract from its grace. In other words, it should remain entirely spontaneous. For the man who asks for favors does not acquire them for a paltry fee, nor does the one who is asked for them bestow them for a small price. So you should buy all your commodities rather than beg for them.

This precept is something that is, I think, especially applicable to matters of honor. He who obtains what he asks for by taking considerable trouble to do so owes himself one debt of gratitude. But he who obtains it without going to the trouble of canvassing owes a double debt to those who bestowed the favor on him: because he has not sought it and because he has obtained it.

Therefore I owe you double thanks, indeed manifold thanks, which I indeed shall proclaim everywhere and always. For the moment, I shall publicly profess my thanks, as is my custom, from a book suitable for this honor (the book is not yet finished). For there is an established order in which a philosopher should return thanks for a statue that has been set up in his honor at public expense. From that order the book will vary only a little according to the standard that Aemilianus Strabo demands. I hope I shall be able to write this kind of book in suitable style. It will be enough today to make only an attempt at it in your company. For Aemilianus is so accomplished in his studies that he is more distinguished by his own talents than by his nobility and consulship.

With what words, Aemilianus Strabo, man of all men, as many as there have ever been or are or will ever be, most illustrious among the best, most learned among both kinds—with what words, I say, shall I render and record thanks to you for your feelings toward me? With what worthy scheme shall I celebrate your praiseworthy kindness, with what recompense of speech shall I equal the renown of your deeds? As Hercules is witness, I swear I have not found the way! But I shall seek and strive unceasingly to find it, "so long as I am mindful of myself, so long as breath rules these limbs."[16] For at this moment—and I

16. *Aeneid* 4.336.

shall not deny it—joy chokes off my eloquence, pleasure impedes my thought. My mind, seized by delights, prefers to rejoice in the present rather than to proclaim what it feels! What shall I do? I want to seem grateful, but joy leaves me no space to express my thanks. May no one, absolutely no one of those wretches desire to upbraid me because I have no less earned my honor than because I have a sense of what it is worth; because I exult in such a testimony from the most illustrious and learned of all men. Indeed, he, a man of consular rank, has given testimony in my behalf in the senate of Carthage—a city whose citizens are no less brilliant than they are immensely kind. He whom it is the highest honor merely to know has stood before the first citizens of Africa to sing my praise.

For I learned the day before yesterday that in his request he asked for a well-frequented spot for my statue. First of all he mentioned the ties of friendship that exist between us; they had their honorable beginning when he and I were fellow students under the same teachers. Then afterward he recounted all my prayers that had attended every step of progress in his official career. This is his first kindness, that he mentions himself as a fellow student with me. Behold now a second one: such a man as this declares that he is beloved by an equal! Moreover, he has recalled that statues and other honors have also been decreed for me in other countries and cities. What can be added to this eulogy from a man of consular rank? Yet he has also noted that the priesthood that I have taken up has conferred on me the highest honor of Carthage. Now this is an exceptional service and one surpassing by far all the others, that he, a most reliable witness, has commended me to you with his own favorable testimony. Finally, he has promised that he himself will erect a statue to me at Carthage—he, a man to whom all provinces and countries everywhere delight in setting up statues of chariots with four and six horses.

What more, then, is there to add to this base and support of my honor? What more for the culmination of my praise? Why, indeed, what remains? Aemilianus Strabo, a man of consular rank, soon by the desires of everyone to be a proconsul, pronounced his opinion about my honors in the senate of Carthage,

and everyone has followed his advice. Does not this seem to you
to be a decree of the senate?

But there is still more. All the Carthaginians who were present
in that most august senate that day willingly decreed that there
be a place provided for a statue. The effect of this was that a
second statue would be provided for by vote of the next senate.
Their veneration for a man of consular rank and their reverence
for him were left intact: they would seem not so much to rival
his deed as to follow it. In a word, a public benefaction would be
decreed for me after a full day's deliberation. Moreover, those
excellent magistrates and most kindly disposed leaders of the
state remembered that what they wanted was prescribed for
them by you. Could I not know this? Could I cease to speak of it?
I would be ungrateful if I did! Quite to the contrary, I feel and I
express the greatest possible thanks to your entire order for
these exceedingly abundant tributes to me. You have honored
me with a most glorious acclamation in your senate house, in
which even to be mentioned by name is the highest of honors.

Therefore, what was reckoned difficult to realize, what was in
truth arduous to do—to be grateful to the people, to please the
senate, to win approval from the magistrates and most prominent citizens—this, if I may speak without vaunting myself, has
somehow now befallen me. What then is lacking for a statue in
my honor except the price of the bronze and the work of the
artist? These are things I have never lacked, even in cities of a
lesser order than yours.[17] May they never fail me in Carthage, a
city where its most illustrious senate is accustomed rather to
pass decrees on important questions than to compute how much
they cost! On this topic I shall speak in a more finished way
when you have finished what you are undertaking. But for you,
noble senators, illustrious citizens, honorable friends: for the
dedication of my statue I shall soon express my thanks more
fully and entrust them to a book, so that throughout all the
provinces it may go and from thence throughout all the world
and for all time render praises of your kindness among peoples
everywhere, throughout all the years.

17. Cf. the dedicatory inscription discovered at Madauros, quoted in Chapter 4.

APPENDIX 2

Two Prayers to Typhon from the Great Magical Papyrus

For Apuleius and the audiences who first heard *The Golden Ass*, magic was no mere superstition that could never exist in the real world. It could be a religion in its own right, with its own cults and appropriate rituals. To pervert the natural order of the world, to cast love spells, to avenge enemies: all these were possible through the supernatural arts practiced by Lucius' voracious hostess, Pamphile. Furthermore, although Seth-Typhon is not called by name in the novel (cf. 11.6), his power is obviously a counterforce opposed to Isis and those who worship her. Magic is one of the two magnetic poles in *The Golden Ass*; between it and the true religion of Isis move all the figures in the novel; each is charged with either the negative force of magic or the positive force of Egyptian (Isiac) religion. Much of the rhetorical force of Apuleius' work derives from this duality of good and evil powers. Escape from the world of magic inspires Lucius' prayer to the Queen of Heaven (11.2) and his speech of thanksgiving to Isis (11.25).

We may well wonder what it was like to worship Typhon and practice magic. Neither the *Apology* nor *The Golden Ass* tells us much. The *Apology* was written to acquit its author of the charge of practicing magic, and presumably it did so. In the novel, magic is a horrific Thessalian craft, which Lucius happily flees forever. Once we have put those two works aside, it may be hard for us to imagine how magic could appeal to any sensible person. Lucius' fascination seems too innocent to be credible.

But we must be wary of modern skepticism. There *were* advantages to practicing magic—or at least many people in antiquity thought there were. These advantages enabled magic to compete with respectable religions for the attention of such a civilized man as Lucius. Fortunately the Greek magical papyri provides a glimpse of the other side of this religious coin. They were recovered at various times from the sands of Egypt and were ultimately collected and edited by the German papyrologist Karl Preisendanz.[1] None of the spells and formulas in the papyri rises to the stylistic level of Apuleius' prose. Save for other sophists, few writers of his time could have equaled him. The importance of the papyri lies in a direction other than literature. Like Isidorus' hymn to Isis in Appendix 3, the magical papyri give us a rare glimpse into popular religious practices—in this instance, rituals of a negative, "demonic" sort.

The following passages are selections from the Great Magical Papyrus, a Greek manuscript now in the Bibliothèque Nationale, Paris.[2] The papyrus itself has been dated to the beginning of the fourth century A.D. It contains prayers and spells that must certainly have been composed before that time. Both selections are notable for their practical instructions and extended passages of magical jargon. The recipes and abracadabra will give the reader some sense of those magical arts that Lucius so longed to acquire and of which Apuleius himself professed to have no knowledge.

1: A Prayer to Achieve Communication with Typhon[3]

Nephotes sends greetings to Psammetichus, king of Egypt, who lives forever.

Since the great god has appointed you as a king who lives forever and nature has made you an excellently wise man, I, too, who wish to show you my industry, have sent you this magic spell, which with the greatest ease achieves a holy efficacy; if you test it, you will wonder at the marvel of this process. You

1. Karl Preisendanz, ed., *Papyri Graecae Magicae: Die griechischen Zauberpapyri;* 2d ed., ed. Albert Henrichs (Stuttgart, 1973–1974).
2. Ibid., IV. 155–221 (pp. 76–79) and IV. 261–285 (pp. 80–81).
3. Communication with a god (the Greek is *systasis*) is sought for personal protection or favors.

will look through a dish for personal vision of divinity, wherein—on whatever day or night you wish, in whatever place you wish—you will see the god in the water and take in a voice from the god in oracular verses that you desire.[4] You will also know the ruler of the world, and if you should propose anything else, he will inform you about other things about which you ask. You will enjoy success by inquiring in this way. First of all, unite yourself with Helios in the following manner. At whatever sunrise you prefer—so long as it is the third day of the moon—climb up to the roof of a house and spread a pure muslin on the floor. Do this in the company of a mystagogue. As for yourself, wreath your brow with black ivy, and when the sun is in the middle of the sky, in the fifth hour, lay yourself down face up, naked, upon the muslin, and order your eyes to be covered with a black band, and wrap yourself up like a dead person, keeping your eyes shut, your face turned toward the sun, and begin with these words:

PRAYER. Mighty Typhon, holder of the scepter and ruler of the kingdom on high, god of gods, lord [*Aberamenthôou* formula], shaker of the shadows, bringer of thunder, bringer of tempests, bringer of lightning in the night, breather of hot and cold gusts, shatterer of rocks, shaker of walls, raiser of waves, shaker and mover of the deep![5]

Iôerbêt au tauï mêni![6]

I am he who searched the whole world with you and found the great Osiris, whom I then clapped into fetters and brought to you; I am he who at your side fought with the gods (others say, "against the gods");[7] I am he who shut the twin folding doors of heaven and put to sleep the serpent on which no man may look; who stopped the sea, the streams, the currents of the rivers, until you were lord over this kingdom. I, your warrior, am overpowered by the gods, I am hurled to the ground through vain anger. Raise, I beseech you, your friend, I entreat you, and do not hurl me to earth, Lord of the Gods.

aeminaebarôtherrethôrabeanimea![8]

4. The ceremony is called *leikanomanteia*, or "dish-divination."
5. Typhon's power to reverse the natural order of things may be compared with the feats of Meroe (1.8).
6. The first of many magic words.
7. This is an alternate reading supplied by Nephotes (or a scribe).
8. Note the palindrome.

Give me power, I entreat you, and grant me this favor, that, whenever I call upon one of the gods themselves to come, he come as quickly as he can at my incantations and that he show himself to me. *Naïne basanaptatou eaptou mênôphaesmê paptou mênôph, aesimê, trauapti, peuchrê, trauara, ptoumêph, mourai, anchouchaphapta, moursa, aramei, Iaô, aththarauï mênoker, boroptoumêth, at tauï mêni charchara, ptoumau, lalapsa, trauï trauepse mamô phortoucha, aeêio iou oeôa, eaï aeêi ôi iaô aêi ai iaô!*

When you have said that three times, there will be this sign of communication with the god (but you, armored as you are with your magic soul, do not be afraid): a sea-hawk will fly down and with his wings strike you on your body, making it clear by this action that you should raise yourself up. Then stand and robe yourself with white dress and set uncut incense drop by drop on a censing altar made of earth, and say this:

I have communed with your holy image, I am empowered by your holy name, I have partaken of your outflow of blessings, master, god of gods, lord, divine spirit, *aththouïn thouthouï tauanti, laô aptatô.*

When you have performed all this, come down in possession of godlike magic power for your own vision of god through dish-divination, and for the raising of the dead as well.

2: Fill In the Blanks

Toward sunup say:

I call on you, who earliest among the gods do wield your weapon; you, who hold the royal scepter over those in heaven; you, master Typhon, above us among the stars; you, the dread lord over the firmaments; you, the object of terror, trembling, and shuddering; you, the clear, the irrestible, the hater of evil; I call on you, Typhon, in hours without law and measure; you, who have walked upon fire that is unquenchable and crackling; you, who are above snow and beneath dark ice. I call upon you who have royal power over the Fates whom men implore, almighty one. Perform for me the things I ask you to, and straightaway concede and permit them to happen for me, as I swear to you *gar thala, bauzau, thôrthôr kathaukath, ïathin, na borkakar, borba, karborboch, mô zau ouzônz, ôn, aubith!* Greatest Typhon, hear me, ———, and carry out for me ———.[9] For I say your true names: *Iôerbêth, Iôpakerbêth, Iôbolchosêth, oen Typhôn, asbarabô, bieaisê, me nerô, maramô, tauêr, chthenthônie, alam bêtôr, menkechra, saueiôr rêseiodôta, abrêsioa, phôthêr, therthônax; nerdômeu, amôrês, meeme, ôiês, suschie, anthônie, Phrâ!* Hear me and carry out ———.

9. More literally, the prayer says "(Name)" and "(the proposed deed)"; the magician's name and the object of his prayer would replace these indefinite words.

A Hymn to Isis
by Isidorus

This hexameter hymn was incised in stone in the late Hellenistic period in Egypt, in the second or first century B.C., by Isidorus. His name means "Isis' gift" and may have been a sobriquet used within the cult. Isidorus' prayer should be compared with Lucius' prayer to the Queen of Heaven at the opening of Book 11 and the self-predication of Isis that follows (11.2 and 5–6). The translation is from Vera Frederika Vanderlip, *The Four Greek Hymns of Isidorus and the Cult of Isis*, American Studies in Papyrology 12 (Toronto, 1972), 18–19, and is quoted by kind permission of Samuel Stevens Hakkert and Company.

HYMN I

O wealth-giver, Queen of the gods, Hermouthis,[1] Lady,
Omnipotent Agathe Tyche,[2] greatly renowned Isis,
Deo,[3] highest Discoverer of all life,
manifold miracles were Your care that You might bring
livelihood to mankind and morality to all;
(and) You taught customs that justice might in some measure prevail;
You gave skills that men's life might be comfortable,
and You discovered the blossoms that produce edible vegetation.
Because of You heaven and the whole earth have their being;
And the gusts of the winds and the sun with its sweet light.
By Your power the channels of Nile are filled, every one,

1. *Hermouthis* is the Greek transliteration of the name of an ancient Egyptian nurse and harvest goddess.
2. Agathe Tyche (Good Fortune) is equated with Isis.
3. Another name for Demeter.

At the harvest season and its most turbulent water is poured
On the whole land that produce may be unfailing.
All mortals who live on the boundless earth,
Thracians, Greeks and Barbarians,
Express Your fair Name, a Name greatly honoured among all, (but)
Each (speaks) in his own language, in his own land.
The Syrians call You: Astarte, Artemis, Nanaia,[4]
The Lycian tribes call You: Leto, the Lady,
The Thracians also name You as Mother of the gods,
And the Greeks (call You) Hera of the Great Throne, Aphrodite,
Hestia the goodly, Rheia and Demeter.
But the Egyptians call You 'Thiouis' (because they know) that You,
     being One, are all
Other goddesses invoked by the races of men.[5]
Mighty One, I shall not cease to sing of Your great Power,
Deathless Saviour, many-named, mightiest Isis,
Saving from war, cities and all their citizens:
Men, their wives, possessions, and children.
As many as are bound fast in prison, in the power of death,
As many as are in pain through long, anguished, sleepless nights,
All who are wanderers in a foreign land,
And as many as sail on the Great Sea in winter
When men may be destroyed and their ships wrecked and sunk...
All (these) are saved if they pray that You be present to help.
Hear my prayers, O One Whose Name has great Power;
Prove Yourself merciful to me and free me from all distress.

Isidorus
wrote (it)

4. An ancient goddess of the Near East.
5. *Thiouis* transliterates a Coptic and Egyptian word, and means "the one."

Select Bibliography

This is not a complete bibliographical survey on Apuleius but only a list of the more important and useful books and articles. A reasonably complete bibliography can be compiled by reference to Margaretha Molt, *Ad Apulei Madaurensis Metamorphoseon Librum Primum Commentarius Exegeticus* (Groningen, 1938), and to the surveys of Carl Schlam (1971) and Gerald Sandy (1974), which are included in the list that follows.

Abt, Adam. *Die Apologie des Apuleius von Madaura und die antike Zauberei.* Giessen, 1908.

Anderson, Graham. *Studies in Lucian's Comic Fiction.* Leiden, 1976.

Aubin, Paul. *Le Problème de la "conversion."* Paris, 1963.

Baldwin, Barry. *Studies in Aulus Gellius.* Lawrence, Kans., 1975.

Barnes, T. D. *Tertullian: An Historical and Literary Study.* Oxford, 1971.

Beaujeu, Jean. *Apuleé: Opuscules philosophiques.* Paris, 1973.

———. "Sérieux et frivolité au IIe siècle de notre ère: Apulée." *Bulletin de l'association Guillaume Budé* 4 (1975), 83–97.

Behr, C. A. *Aelius Aristides and the Sacred Tales.* Chicago, 1969.

Bernhard, Max. *Der Stil des Apuleius von Madaura: Ein Beitrag zur Stilistik des Spätlateins.* Stuttgart, 1927.

Binder, Gerhard, and Reinhold Merkelbach. *Amor und Psyche.* Darmstadt, 1968.

Bompaire, Jacques. *Lucien écrivain: Imitation et création.* Paris, 1958.

Bonner, S. F. *Roman Declamation.* Liverpool, 1949.

Bowersock, G. W. *Greek Sophists in the Roman Empire.* Oxford, 1969.

———, ed. *Approaches to the Second Sophistic.* Papers presented at the 105th annual meeting of the American Philological Association, University park, Pa., 1974.

Brock, M. Dorothy. *Studies in Fronto and His Age.* Cambridge, 1911.

Brotherton, Blanche. "The Introduction of Characters by Name in the *Metamorphoses* of Apuleius." *Classical Philology* 29 (1934), 36–52.

Butler, H. E., and A. S. Owen. *Apulei Apologia.* Oxford, 1914.

Callebat, Louis. *Sermo cotidianus dans les Métamorphoses d'Apulée.* Paris, 1968.

Cumont, Franz. *Oriental Religions in Roman Paganism.* New York, 1956.

Dillon, John. *The Middle Platonists.* Ithaca, N.Y., 1977.

Dodds, E. R. *Pagan and Christian in an Age of Anxiety.* Cambridge, 1965.

Drake, Gertrude. "Candidus: A Unifying Theme in Apuleius' *Metamorphoses.*" *Classical Journal* 64 (1968), 102–109.

Fehling, Detlev. *Amor und Psyche: Die Schöpfung des Apuleius und ihre Einwirkung auf das Märchen, eine Kritik der romantischen Märchen Theorie.* Mainz, 1977.

Festugière, A. J. *La révélation d'Hermès Trismégiste.* Vol. 3, *Les doctrines de l'âme.* Paris, 1953.

Fredouille, Jean-Claude. *Apulée: Métamorphoses Livre XI.* Paris, 1975.

Graves, Robert, trans. *The Transformations of Lucius, Otherwise Known as The Golden Ass.* London, 1950.

Griffiths, J. Gwyn. *Plutarch's De Iside et Osiride.* Cardiff, 1970.

———. *Apuleius of Madauros: The Isis-Book (Metamorphoses, Book XI).* Leiden, 1975.

Grimal, Pierre. *Metamorphoseis 4.28–6.24: Le conte d'Amour et Psyche.* Paris, 1963.

Heine, Rolf. "Untersuchungen zur Romanform des Apuleius von Madaura." Ph.D. thesis, University of Göttingen, 1962.

Helm, Rudolf. *Apulei opera quae supersunt.* Vol. 1, *Metamorphoseon libri xi,* 3d ed., Leipzig, 1955; vol. 2, pt. 1, *Apologia (De Magia),* 2d ed., Leipzig, 1959; vol. 2, pt. 2, *Florida,* Leipzig, 1959.

Junghanns, Paul. "Die Erzählungstechnik von Apuleius' Metamorphosen und ihrer Vorlage." *Philologus,* suppl. 24, vol. 1. Leipzig, 1932.

Kennedy, George. *The Art of Persuasion in Greece.* Princeton, N.J., 1963.

———. *The Art of Rhetoric in the Roman World.* Princeton, N.J., 1972.

Kenny, Brendan. "The Reader's Role in the *Golden Ass.*" *Arethusa* 7 (1974), 197–209.

Leeman, A. D. *Orationis ratio.* Amsterdam, 1963.

Lindsay, Jack. *The Golden Ass of Apuleius.* New York, 1932; Bloomington, Ind., 1962.

Luck, Georg. *Hexen und Zauberei in der römischen Dichtung.* Zurich, 1962.

Macleod, M. D. *Lucian.* Loeb Classical Library, vol. 8. London, 1967. (Contains text and translation of *Lucius or the Ass.*)

Mason, H. J. "Lucius at Corinth." *Phoenix* 25 (1971), 160–165.

Médan, Pierre. *La latinité d'Apulée dans les Métamorphoses*. Paris, 1926.

Merkelbach, Reinhold. *Roman und Mysterium in der Antike*. Munich, 1962.

Neumann, Erich. *Amor and Psyche: The Psychic Development of the Feminine*. Princeton, N.J., 1956.

Nilsson, Martin P. *Geschichte der griechischen Religion: Die hellenistische und römische Zeit*. Hanbuch der Altertumswissenschaft, pt. 5, vol. 2. 2d ed. Munich, 1961.

Nock, A. D. *Conversion*. Oxford, 1933.

Norden, Eduard. *Die antike Kunstprosa*. Leipzig and Berlin, 1923.

Oldfather, W. A., H. V. Canter, and B. E. Perry. *Index Apuleianus*. Middletown, Conn., 1934.

Opeku, Fabian. "A Commentary with Introduction on the *Florida* of Apuleius." Ph.D. thesis, University of London, 1974.

Penwill, J. L. "Slavish Pleasures and Profitless Curiosity: Fall and Redemption in Apuleius' *Metamorphoses*." *Ramus* 4 (1975), 49–82.

Perry, B. E. *The Ancient Romances: A Literary-Historical Account of Their Origins* (Sather Classical Lectures 37, Berkeley, 1967).

Preisendanz, Karl, ed., *Papyri Graecae Magicae: Die griechischen Zauberpapyri*, 2d ed., ed. Albert Henrichs (Stuttgart, 1973–1974).

Reardon, B. P. "The Greek Novel." *Phoenix* 23 (1969), 291–309.

———. *Courants littéraires grecs des IIe et IIIe siècles après J.-C*. Paris, 1970.

———. "Aspects of the Greek Novel." *Greece and Rome* 23 (1976), 118–131.

Riefstahl, Hermann. *Der Roman des Apuleius*. Frankfurt, 1938.

Robertson, D. S., and Paul Vallette. *Apulée: Les Métamorphoses*. 3 vols. Paris, 1940–1945.

Rohde, Erwin. *Der griechische Roman und seine Vorläufer*. 3d ed. Leipzig, 1914.

Romilly, Jacqueline de. *Magic and Rhetoric in Ancient Greece*. Cambridge, Mass., 1975.

Sandy, Gerald N. "Recent Scholarship on the Prose Fiction of Classical Antiquity." *Classical World* 67 (1974), 321–360.

———. "*Serviles Voluptates* in Apuleius' *Metamorphoses*." *Phoenix* 28 (1974), 234–244.

Schlam, Carl C. "The Curiosity of the *Golden Ass*." *Classical Journal* 64 (1968), 120–125.

———. "The Scholarship on Apuleius since 1938." *Classical World* 64 (1971), 285–309.

———. *Cupid and Psyche: Apuleius and the Monuments*. University Park, Pa., 1976.

Scobie, Alexander. *Apuleius Metamorphoses (Asinus Aureus)*. Bk. 1. *A Commentary*. Meisenheim am Glan, 1975.

Stanford, W. B. *The Ulysses Theme*. 2d ed. Oxford, 1963.

Sullivan, J. P. *The Satyricon of Petronius: A Literary Study*. London, 1968.

Swahn, J. Ö. *The Tale of Cupid and Psyche*. Lund, 1975.

Tatum, James. "The Tales of Apuleius' *Metamorphoses*." *Transactions and Proceedings of the American Philological Association* 100 (1969), 487–527.

———. "Apuleius and Metamorphosis." *American Journal of Philology* 93 (1972), 306–313.

Thiel, Helmut van. *Der Eselsroman*. Vol. 1, *Untersuchungen*; vol. 2, *Synoptische Ausgabe*. Munich, 1971–1972.

Thomas, P. *Apulei Platonici Madaurensis opera quae supersunt*. Vol. 3, *De philosophia libri*. Stuttgart, 1970.

Trenkner, Sophie. *The Greek Novella in the Classical Period*. Cambridge, 1958.

Vallette, Paul. *Apuleé: Apologie, Florides*. 2d ed. Paris, 1960.

Vanderlip, Vera F. *The Four Greek Hymns of Isidorus and the Cult of Isis*. American Studies in Papyrology 12. Toronto, 1972.

Walsh, P. G. *The Roman Novel: The Satyricon of Petronius and the Metamorphoses of Apuleius*. Cambridge, 1970.

Wissowa, Georg. *Religion und Kultus der Römer*. Handbuch der klassichen Altertumswissenschaft. pt. 5, vol. 4. Munich, 1902.

Witt, R. E. *Isis in the Greco-Roman World*. London, 1971.

Wittmann, Willi. *Das Isisbuch des Apuleius*. Stuttgart, 1938.

Wlosok, Antonie. "Zur Einheit der Metamorphosen des Apuleius." *Philologus* 113 (1969), 68–84.

———. "Amor and Cupido," *Harvard Studies in Classical Philology* 79 (1975), 165–179.

General Index

Achilles, 33, 79
Achilles Tatius, 42, 63
Actaeon, 37, 38, 136
Adrian of Phoenicia (sophist), 116
Adultery. *See* Motifs.
Aemilianus, Sicinius, 112, 113
Aemilianus Strabo (proconsul), 110–11, 175–77
Aeneas, 60, 89
Aesop's fables, 101, 103
African Latin, 142
Agricola (in Tacitus), 109–10
Albinus, Clodius, 98–99
Alcimus, 48–49
Allegory. *See* Narrative techniques.
Anubis, 82
Aphrodite, 50, 93. *See also* Venus.
Apollonius of Tyana, 114, 127
Apology (Apuleius), 105–19, 178
Apuleius
  allusions to, in *Golden Ass*, 19, 88, 112
  chronology of, 17, 110–12
  criticisms of, 19, 23, 33–34, 62, 102–3
  education of, 17–18, 114, 125–26, 169–70
  faith of, 129–30
  and Gorgias, 141
  literary activities of, 95–96, 136, 141, 167–68, 169–70
  marriage of, 112–13
  occasional verses of, 117
  performances of, as sophist, 122–34
  as philosopher, 64, 105–10, 130–33
  public honors of, 108, 171–77
  public offices of, 110
  trial of, 40, 110–19
Aretalogies, 32, 154–59, 183–84. *See*

also Composition; Isis; Language and style.
Aristides, Aelius, 18, 123, 127, 129, 174
Aristides of Miletus, 96, 97, 102
Aristomenes, 24, 27, 28, 34, 36, 37, 42
Aristophanes, 60
Aristotle, 128, 137
Asclepiades (physician), 78, 165–66
Asinus aureus. See Golden Ass, The.
Ass
  characteristics of, in folktales, 47
  as symbol, 30, 43–47
Athena, 75–76, 122
Athens, 18, 112, 125
Auerbach, Erich, 37
Augustine, St., 99–100, 105–6, 112, 131
Aurelius, Marcus, 64, 142, 143, 171

Barbarus, 74–75
Boccaccio, Giovanni, 11, 75
Butler, H. E., 163
Byrrhena, 37, 38, 39

Candidus, 34
Carneades, 110
Carthage, 18, 125, 126, 127, 174–77
Catullus, 117
Cenchreae, 23, 80, 82
Cerdo, 39, 146
Character, symbolized by metamorphosis, 29–32
Characterization
  in *Apology*, 114
  in *Golden Ass*, 149
  See also names of individual characters.
Charite, 31, 32, 62–63, 69, 93, 146, 148–49. *See also* Plotina.
Chariton, 42

Index of Passages Cited

APULEIUS AND

The Golden Ass

Designed by Richard Rosenbaum.
Composed by The Composing Room of Michigan, Inc.
in 10 point VIP Palatino, 2 points leaded,
with display lines in Palatino
Printed offset by Thomson/Shore, Inc. on
Warren's Number 66 Antique Offset.
Bound by John H. Dekker & Sons, Inc.
in Holliston book cloth
and stamped in All Purpose foil.

Library of Congress Cataloging in Publication Data
(For library cataloging purposes only)

Tatum, James.
  Apuleius and The golden ass.

  Bibliography: p.
  Includes index.
  1. Apuleius, Madaurensis. Metamorphoses.
I. Title.
PA6217.T3   873'.01   78-74220
ISBN 0-8014-1163-7